C. Elvin Haupt

Stories from Bible History for Home and School.

C. Elvin Haupt

Stories from Bible History for Home and School.

ISBN/EAN: 9783337171988

Printed in Europe, USA, Canada, Australia, Japan

Cover: Foto ©Lupo / pixelio.de

More available books at **www.hansebooks.com**

STORIES

FROM

BIBLE HISTORY,

FOR

HOME AND SCHOOL.

"Behold the Lamb of God."

"Suffer little children, and forbid them not, to come unto me."

READING, PA.
PILGER PUBLISHING HOUSE.
1885.

Entered according to Act of Congress in the year 1884
by
AUGUSTUS BENDEL.
In the Office of the Librarian of Congress at Washington.

BY WAY OF INTRODUCTION.

One of the greatest defects manifest in our days is the lack of home and school Instruction in the Bible History. Vast and wide spread ignorance exists concerning the facts, persons, places and sequences of the Ante-Mosaic, Israelitish and New Testament activity. This little book, of elements and rudimentary facts, has been prepared to aid parents and teachers in the development of the soul of the child by the study of the pure depths of holy History. Though it is intended to guide the child-mind along the path of the sacred Narrative, it cannot be denied that the chief thoughts and widest unfoldings of its Record cluster around the manifestation of the Person, and the declaration of the Mediatorial Wonder-work of our adorable, true and only Redeemer, Jesus Christ.

To achieve the very best results, for the child, both memorizing and reviewing are necessary. It is earnestly hoped that teachers will first see that the verses to be committed are recited from memory, and discover whether the passages of Scripture, [or marked portions thereof,] have been read in preparation during the previous week. The book has been so arranged that five lessons are given to reviewing, during the year. This volume may be used at home, or school as one of a series of graded text books, either simultaneously with others, or consecutively. But no child should be promoted unless it knows the facts of the book it lays aside.

The "Story" is the children's part of the lesson. It should be read aloud attentively, either by each reciting a part, or in concert. The "Review" and "Notes" are intended to assist the teacher. The Story of the day having been read, let the teacher begin to question from the children all the facts they have learned, and draw for them whatever lessons are suggested. The queries given are merely intended as leaders to the subject; leaving to the teacher to interpose any others that may be deemed proper. If a difficult word contained in the lesson is not found in the foot-notes of the page it may doubtless be explained more fully elsewhere; as seen in the Index.

As more than 750 Bible words and terms have been explained by the Notes, the Index to these will form a concise Bible Dictionary for all those whose resources are limited.

Illustrations, as a relief to the eye and mind, have been added, wherever possible.

Though the Book has been arranged to follow the Christian Year, it may be begun at any time, or, if preferred the Second Half may be used during the earlier portion of the year; leaving to the Sundays after Trinity, the Stories of the Old Testament.

With an earnest prayer that the vitalizing power of the Saviour's life may be shed abroad into every heart, and that all the flock of the good Shepherd may learn to follow Him, this humble effort, prepared during days of busy pastoral life, is lovingly offered to His Church.

C. ELVIN HOUPT.

Grace Parsonage, Lancaster, Pa.
EASTER MONDAY, March 26. 1883.

CONTENTS.

PART 1. THE OLD TESTAMENT HISTORY.

1.	THE CREATION	5
2.	THE FALL. CAIN AND ABEL	6
3.	ENOCH	8
4.	NOAH AND THE FLOOD	9
5.	THE TOWER OF BABEL	12
6.	ABRAHAM	13
7.	ISAAC	16
8.	ESAU AND JACOB	18
9.	JOSEPH AND HIS BRETHREN	20
10.	JOSEPH AND HIS BRETHREN [II.]	22
11.	JOB	25
12.	REVIEW	27
13.	MOSES AND AARON	29
14.	MOSES AND AARON [II]	33
15.	THE TABERNACLE	37
16.	JOSHUA	40
17.	THE JUDGES	44
18.	RUTH	48
19.	SAMUEL	50
20.	KING SAUL	53
21.	KING DAVID	56
22.	KING SOLOMON	60
23.	THE LATER KINGS	64
24.	REVIEW	67
25.	MORDECAI AND ESTHER	69
26.	THE CAPTIVITY AND LATER HISTORY	71
27.	THE TEMPLES OF ISRAEL	75
28.	THE PROPHETS AND TYPES OF CHRIST	77

PART 2. THE NEW TESTAMENT HISTORY.

29.	JOHN THE BAPTIST AND HIS MESSAGE	85
30.	THE COMING AND CHILDHOOD OF JESUS THE CHRIST	88
31.	THE BAPTISM AND TEMPTATION OF JESUS	93
32.	OUR LORD TEACHING AND SENDING FORTH HIS DISCIPLES	96

33.	THE MIRACLES OF JESUS..	99
34.	THE TRANSFIGURATION OF JESUS...	103
35.	THE SUFFERINGS AND DEATH OF JESUS..	106
36.	THE RISING OF JESUS FROM DEATH..	113
37.	THE DEPARTURE OF JESUS...	117
38.	REVIEW...	120
39.	THE COMING OF THE HOLY SPIRIT...	123
40.	PERSECUTION AND IMPRISONMENT..	125
41.	THE DEACONS,—STEPHEN AND THE PERSECUTION....................................	127
42.	PHILIP TEACHING SAMARIA AND THE EUNUCH.......................................	129
43.	THE GREAT CHANGE IN SAUL..	132
44.	THE JOURNEY OF PETER..	135
45.	BARNABAS, PAUL AND MARK, THE MISSIONARIES....................................	139
46.	THE COUNCIL AT JERUSALEM AND THE EPISTLES....................................	142
47.	THE MISSIONARIES, PAUL, SILAS AND TIMOTHY....................................	144
48.	PAUL'S THIRD MISSIONARY JOURNEY...	147
49.	PAUL A PRISONER..	150
50.	THE TAKING OF JERUSALEM AND THE BANISHMENT OF ST. JOHN......................	153
51.	REVIEW...	155
52.	A GENERAL REVIEW...	158

PART FIRST.

THE OLD TESTAMENT.

Lesson I. The First Sunday in Advent.

THE CREATION.

Commit to Memory Psalm 124: 8; Acts 17: 24, 25. Read Gen. 1 and 2.

THE STORY.

IT was God who created Heaven and Earth At first all was dark and confused. He made all things in six days. On the first, He made Day and Night. On the second, He divided the Heavens from the Earth. On the third day, He made Seas and dry Land, and made Vegetation grow. On the fourth day, He made the Sun, the Moon and the Stars. On the fifth, He made the Creatures that swim, and Birds. On the sixth day, the Lord God made the land Animals; and at last, of the dust, Adam, the first man; as well as Eve, the first woman, by taking a rib from Adam's side, out of which He formed her. God gave to man his soul, and put Adam and Eve in Eden, a beautiful Garden. All that God made was very good. After God had ended His work of creation, He made the seventh day a holy Sabbath of rest; so that man, keeping holy the Sabbath day, might think of God and love Him.

REVIEW.

Who created you and all things? Apos. Creed, Art. I. Is. 48: 13.
What does "created" mean? Repeat the First Commandment. John 1: 3. Acts 14: 17.
In what condition were all things at first?
In how many days did He make all things?
Can you repeat the Third Commandment? Exod. 20: 8—11.
What did God make on the first day? On the second? On the third? On the fourth? On the fifth? On the sixth?
Can you repeat for me the name of any stone which God made? A plant? A heavenly light? A fish? A bird? A creeping animal? A walking animal? Whose are all these things?
Whom did God make at last? Why do you think, God made man last?
How did God make Eve?
What special gift did God make to man? What is the Soul?
Where did Adam and Eve live?
How did God's Work appear when finished?
Why did God cease from His labor then and bless the seventh day? Mark 2: 27, 28. Exod. 31: 13—17. Lev. 19: 30.
How should we use the Lord's Day?

Notes. ADVENT, coming, approach. CREATED, made from nothing. CONFUSED, out of order. VEGETATION, plants, herbs, shrubs and trees. RIB, a bone of the body. RESTED, ceased to labor. SABBATH, seventh, or rest. SOUL, the part of man which loves God and knows right from wrong.

Lesson 2.—The Second Sunday in Advent.

THE FALL. CAIN AND ABEL.

COMMIT 1. Cor. 15: 21, 22. READ GEN. 3. AND 4: 1—16.

THE STORY.

God taught Adam and Eve to eat of any tree of the Garden, except the tree of the knowledge of good and evil. This, He said, would cause them to die. But Satan, God's proud, disobedient, fallen angel, came to Eve as if he was a beautiful serpent. He told her a lie, saying, "Ye shall not surely die," but be like God, knowing good and evil, if you disobey and eat the forbidden fruit. Eve did eat. She gave to Adam and he also ate of the fruit. This was sin. Then God punished them. He sent a good angel to drive them out of Eden, into a land of thorns and sorrow. Two sons, Cain and Abel, were born. Cain grew to be a gardener and Abel a shepherd. Selfish Cain feared God,

THE FALL. CAIN AND ABEL.

Abel loved Him. God was pleased with Abel. But jealous Cain killed Abel. Cain must go away. So sin and death were in the world, and had passed into all men. But to Adam and Eve, God promised a Saviour, who some day would appear.

The Fall.

REVIEW.

What was said by the LORD to our first parents?
Of what tree were they forbidden to eat?
Had they their choice to eat, or not to eat?
Why did God forbid them this fruit?
In what form did Satan appear? Who is Satan?
What did he say to Eve?
Can you name three sins that Eve and Adam committed? Prov. 16:18. 17:4. Phil. 4:11. James 1:13—15.
Did God know this? Num. 32:23. Prov. 15:3.
Why did God punish them? How did He do it? Gen. 3:23, 24.
Who were the first children on earth?
What work did Cain and Abel do?
How did Cain feel toward God? How did Abel serve God?
Why, do you think, God loved Abel?

Cain and Abel.

How did Cain treat Abel? 1. John 3: 12, 15. Why?
What must Cain do?
What were shown to be in the world? Rom. 7: 23—25.
Are all men sinners? Rom. 5: 12. Who was promised? Gen. 3: 15.

Notes. FALL, a going down to destruction. PERMITTED, allowed. SATAN, the devil, God's enemy, man's destroyer. DISOBEDIENT, not doing what we are told. PROUD, self loving, haughty. LIE, that which is not true. FORBIDDEN, not for us to have, do, or use. SIN, breaking God's law. PUNISHED, caused to suffer for doing wrong. SORROW, regret. JEALOUS, full of envy.

Lesson 3.—The Third Sunday in Advent.

ENOCH.

COMMIT HEBREWS 11: 5, 6. READ GEN. 5: 18—27.

THE STORY.

Adam had another son named Seth. He had many descendants. Of these, one, in the seventh generation from Adam, was

Enoch the father of Methusaleh. People lived long then; and Methusaleh who was the oldest man, lived for nine hundred and sixty nine years. Enoch was very Godlike and pious. He walked on earth with God and was full of faith. This was well pleasing to God. Indeed so great was his faith that God permitted him to know of the Second Coming of the Lord Jesus. After a life on earth of 365 years, God took Enoch to heaven without dying.

REVIEW.

Can you tell me the name of another son of Adam?
Mention a man of the seventh generation from Adam.
Of whom was he the father?
How long did Methusaleh live?
Tell me about Enoch's life? Matt. 5: 16.
What is faith in God? Phil. 1: 6.
Does faith please God? Ps. 40: 4. St. Luke 1: 45. Rom. 5: 1. Gal. 3: 9.
Does faith save souls? Acts 16: 31.
Of what great fact did Enoch's faith teach him? Jude 14: 15.
What was remarkable about the close of his life? Heb. 11: 5.
Who took Enoch?
How long had he lived?
Should not we all believe in God and follow our Saviour? Prov. 3: 5. St. John 3: 16. 14: 1.
Is a good life a happy and useful one?

Notes. DESCENDANTS, children of a family, posterity. GENERATION, brothers and sisters of one family. GODLIKE, trying to be like God. PIOUS, having respect for God. FAITH, trust, dependence. PLEASING, agreeable, suitable, satisfactory. SECOND COMING, the return of Jesus to this world, for the judgment of all men. (See II. Article of the Creed.)

Lesson 4.—The Fourth Sunday in Advent.

NOAH AND THE FLOOD.

COMMIT HEBREWS 11: 7. READ GEN. 6—9.

THE STORY.

Enoch's great-grandson was Noah. The world had become corrupt and wicked. But Noah was faithful; and taught his wife with Shem, Ham and Japheth, (his three sons) and their wives, to love and obey the LORD. God determined to destroy

Noah and the Flood.

the wicked worldlings, and sent rain for 40 days and 40 nights, with a great flood, ("Deluge") over the earth.

But He had taught Noah to build a great wooden Ark, or floating house; about 550 feet long, 91 feet wide, and 55 feet high. While wicked men laughed, Noah went on building the

The Flood.

Ark. Into this Ark, God sent pairs of every living animal, and seven of each most-needed kind. Noah and his family, (8 in all,) were shut in by the LORD with the animals to be saved. Then the flood came and all outside were drowned. The Ark floated for five months. Then it grounded and began to rest.

NOAH AND THE FLOOD.

In one year and ten days after the flood began, Noah came forth upon Mount Ararat; a mountain more than three miles high. Noah had sent out a raven and twice a dove, to see if it were safe to go forth from the Ark. When finally they all came forth safely, Noah and his children built an Altar to the LORD and offered Sacrifice. And God gave a token of His love in the beautiful Rainbow; and promised never again to destroy the world by a flood.

Noah and his family offering Sacrifice.

REVIEW.

Who was Noah?
What was the state of the world?
But did this make Noah do evil? Heb. 10: 38, 39. Does God love the good?
Who were Noah's sons? How were they taught?
What did God do in punishment of a sinful world? Job 22: 16.
How did He warn Noah? How was he to make his Ark?
Why was it to be so large? What were put into it? Who sent them in?
How many persons were in the ark? How long did they float?
How long did Noah remain in the Ark?
Where did Noah leave the Ark? Ps. 74: 15.
What birds had he sent forth?
What did Noah do on leaving the Ark?
What does the Rainbow mean? Gen. 9: 15—17. How may the Ark teach a beautiful lesson of the Church in Christ? Should we be ashamed if we are doing right? Ought not all be in Christ?

Notes. CORRUPT, made filthy. WICKED, bad, full of sin. FAITHFUL, steady in trust. DETERMINED, resolved. WORLDLINGS, people fond of the worldly ways of sin. ARK, a case or vessel for keeping safely. PAIR, a male and female of each kind of creature. ALTAR, a raised place for worship. SACRIFICE, anything offered to God and consumed on an Altar. TOKEN, sign, proof. DESTROY, spoil, ruin, make useless.

Lesson 5.—Christmas, or the Sunday after Christmas.

THE TOWER OF BABEL.

COMMIT HEBREWS 10: 30. READ GEN. 11: 1—9.

THE STORY.

Noah's descendants journeyed together down from Mount Ararat. They became many and spoke the same language. They came to the beautiful plain of Shinar. Here they thought they would build a Tower, so high, that, if another flood came, they could save themselves; and need not think of God. Thus they so soon forgot God, and were planning only of what *they* could do. The LORD saw that they would grow more willful and wicked. He wisely prevented them from building their Tower. He changed their one language into many. Then the people began to separate and wander into different countries. The place where the Tower was left unfinished is called BABEL;

which means CONFUSION. Sin in men separates them in life on earth but the Coming of Christ to the world is the bond of union in eternal life, bringing together those who were scattered abroad.

REVIEW.

How did God bless Noah's family?
Did all speak alike? Did they journey together? Ps. 133: 1.
At Shinar what did they propose to build? Prov. 16: 21.
Why did they propose to build it?
What had God promised in the Rainbow? Lesson 4. Was this tower needed therefore?
Does this show that they were pious, and remembered God?
What did the LORD see? Prov. 15: 3.
Who only can save us? Deut. 20: 4. Prov. 20: 22. St. Luke 9: 56.
What did the LORD do unto them? How?
Can He do whatever He will? Ps. 115: 3.
Is not the same language a bond of union?
What did this change cause the people to do?
What does the name BABEL mean?
Is the LORD always displeased with wickedness? Prov. 3: 33. Eccles. 8: 12, 13.
Does sin cause men to neglect and forsake one another? Job 15: 34. Prov. 10: 12.
What is the great bond of union among men? ANS. The birth of Jesus Christ. St. John 17: 20, 21

NOTES. CHRISTMAS, the day which reminds us of the birth and Incarnation of Christ. ETERNAL, without an end. LANGUAGE, words, said or written by which our minds can express our wants or ideas. PLAIN, a level land. PREVENTED, stopped, checked in progress. SEPARATE, to go apart. WILLFUL, determined, set in mind, stubborn.

Lesson 6.—New Year or the Sunday after New Year's Day.

ABRAHAM.

COMMIT HEBREWS 11: 8, 9. 10. READ GEN. 11: 25—27.

THE STORY.

Among the descendants of Shem, was Abram. He was very faithful and obedient to God. When Abram was 75 years old, the LORD called him to leave his home and come into the land of Canaan. God promised both to give him that land and that the SAVIOUR should be born in his family. With Sarai, his wife, and Lot, his nephew, he came to Canaan with his flocks around him, and lived in tents. He became very rich. So did Lot. But Lot separated from Abram and went to live in Sodom, a wicked city. Here he was taken captive by enemies of Sodom. Abram with some of his servants came and rescued Lot.

Sarai had no child. Then Ishmael became Abram's child by Hagar, Sarai's Egyptian servant. But such a child was not

Abraham Sacrificing Isaac.

the true child which Abram supposed, as promised of God to him and Sarai.

So, though Abram was 100 years old the LORD gave to Sarai, whom he called "Sarah" or Princess, a son, Isaac, whom Abram circumcised when 8 days old. God now visited him and called him "Abraham," the "father of many nations," and showed him that He would now destroy Sodom and another wicked city Gomorrah.

But Lot was again saved. The LORD told Abraham to take his "child of promise," Isaac, and go, offer him like a lamb as a sacrifice, at Mount Moriah. God was trying Abraham's strong faith and sent an angel to stop Abraham just as he was ready to offer his son. The LORD was pleased with Abraham's faithfulness and showed him a sheep caught, which the father took and offered instead of the child. The LORD greatly blessed pious Abraham and, after a long and useful life of 175 years, he died. He was the founder of the Jewish nation; and thus a type, (or likeness) of CHRIST, the founder of the Church, or "Kingdom of the Lord," for all nations.

REVIEW.

Of what family was Abram? Did he have a true heart toward God? Heb. 11: 17.

What did the LORD command him to do? How old was Abram then?

What did God promise? Gen. 12: 3, 7. 21: 12.

Has He fulfilled it? Matt. 1: 1. Acts 13: 23. Rom. 9: 7. Gal. 3: 13, 14, 29.

Did Abram obey? Heb. 11: 8.

Who came with him?

How did the LORD bless them?

What became of Lot?

Had Abram any children? Who visited Abram? What did He name Abram?

What did God show? Why do you think Sodom and Gomorrah were destroyed?

What strange command did the LORD give Abraham?

What is a sacrifice?

Why did He thus command?

How do we know this?

Of Whom is Abraham a type? Why?

How long did Abraham live?

Notes. OBEDIENT, freely doing one's duty. PROMISED, foretold. CAPTIVE, made a prisoner. RESCUED, helped, set free, saved. CIRCUMCISED, marked in the flesh, as a child of God's law; for God's adoption under His old promise of care and salvation, given to the faithful children of men. Baptism takes its place in the new order of salvation, or the covenant with God. TRY, put to the test. FOUNDER, one who lays the foundation on which others build, or are established. TYPE, an emblem or sign, representing a person or thing to come, a prefiguration. [This will be explained more fully in Lesson 28.]

16　Isaac.

Lesson 7.—The First Sunday in the Epiphany Season.
ISAAC.
Commit Hebrews 11: 17, 18.　Read. Gen. 21—35.
THE STORY.

Isaac, as we have seen was the child of aged Abram and Sarah. Ishmael, the adopted and supposed child of promise was

Hagar and the Angel.

sent away by Abram in the care of Hagar, his mother, Sarah's servant, into a wilderness, where he grew to be a great prince.

When the Lord, to prove Abram, told him to take Isaac and

go to offer him as a sacrifice, he obeyed. Because the LORD found them so faithful, he blessed both the pious father and the son who was willing to be slain.

Abraham did not wish that Isaac should marry one of the daughters of the Canaanites who worshiped idols. So he sent Eliezer his steward to his old home in Chaldea to find a believing wife for his son Isaac.

Eliezer prayed for help to do his work well and God showed him whom to chose. It was Rebekah the daughter of Bethuel Abraham's nephew. Eliezer thanked the LORD, gave Rebekah many gifts and brought the willing maiden with him to the home of Abraham. They arrived at sunset just as Isaac was walking in the field.

Isaac the peace loving young shepherd married Rebekah and became very rich in flocks and herds. His twin sons were Esau and Jacob. In his old age, through blindness and the deception of Jacob, his mother's favorite, he gave to Jacob the chief blessing which belonged to Esau the first born. For this Esau hated Jacob. After a life of 180 years aged Isaac died and was buried by his sons who had become reconciled. Isaac was called the "child of promise" because the promised SAVIOUR was to descend in his family from Abraham.

REVIEW.

What precious promise had the LORD given Abraham?
Who was the mother of the child? What did they name him?
Does God always fulfill His promises? Gen. 21: 1—5. 2. Cor. 1: 20.
Who was Ishmael? Why was he sent away? In whose care?
What became of him?
How did God test Abraham's faith? Did he prove faithful?
Should not we trust in God above everything?
What did Abraham not wish? Why? 1st Com. How did he arrange the matter?
What good example did Eliezer set? St. Luke 12: 42, 43. 16: 10. I. Cor. 4: 1, 2.
Does God hear and answer prayer? Jas. 5: 16.
Whom did Eliezer find and bring?
Having married Rebekah what gentle life did Isaac lead?
Who were their sons? What great mistake did Isaac make?
Should parents love one child more than another?
Does not God love all alike? John 3: 16.
What was the effect of this favoritism?
Were the brothers afterward reconciled? Matt. 18: 22.

Who lived longer, Abraham or Isaac?
Who buried Isaac?
Why was Isaac called the "child of promise?" Gen. 22: 18.

Notes. EPIPHANY, a showing to all, making visible. ADOPTED, taken into a family as a child. WILDERNESS, a wild unused land. SLAIN, put to death. WILLING, cheerfully ready. CANAANITES, idolatrous people of Canaan. [See Map] STEWARD the chief servant of the family. DECEPTION, cheating, lying, hypocrisy. FAVORITE, one loved more than another. HATED, envied, despised, was angry.

Lesson 8.—The Second Sunday in the Epiphany Season.
ESAU AND JACOB.
COMMIT EPHES. 4: 31, 32. READ GEN. 25—50.

THE STORY.

Esau and Jacob were Isaac's twin sons. Esau loved to hunt in the wilderness for game. Jacob was a shepherd. The birthright was Esau's, but Jacob compelled his brother when faint and hungry after hunting to sell it to him for a "mess of pottage." Isaac loved Esau but Rebekah loved Jacob. When Isaac became old and was almost blind, Jacob deceived his father saying that he was Esau. In this way he obtained the blessing of Esau the first born. Esau became very angry. Jacob fled far away to his uncle Laban, Rebekah's brother. On his way Jacob, while resting, had a wonderful dream, about a ladder, or stairway; on which angels were passing down and up. At its top stood the LORD, who promised that the family of Jacob should be a blessing to the world. Jacob called the place of his dream "Bethel," or the House of God.

In Laban's home Jacob served 20 years and married Leah and Rachel, Laban's daughters. He earned many cattle. Then Jacob returned to his father's house and was forgiven by Esau who had become a great man. On the way homeward Jacob wrestled with an angel of God, at Peniel, who blessed him and changed his name to Israel, which signifies "He who prevails with God." Jacob had 12 sons who were called "Children of Israel." Their descendants formed the nation called Hebrews, or Jews.

But, through the jealousy of the other sons Jacob lost Joseph his favorite son and in his old age suffered much from sorrow and famine. He sent his sons down to Egypt to buy a little corn, when behold! Joseph is found again.

Esau and Jacob.

All the family now remove to Egypt where Jacob sees King Pharaoh. Jacob died in Egypt aged 147 years. His sons carried him to Canaan for burial.

REVIEW.

How were Esau and Jacob related?
How did Jacob gain Esau's birthright?
What sins did Jacob commit? See 4th, 8th, 9th and 10th Com.
Did the sin of Jacob make Esau angry? What must Jacob do?
Prov. 28: 1. Isaiah 57: 21.

Was Jacob punished for his youthful **folly in his old age?** Gen. 47: 9.
Do you think that Jacob was sorry for his sins and **turned to God** for forgiveness? Was this right?
What beautiful dream did Jacob have?
What did he call the place of his dream?
Did the LORD promise anything to Jacob at Bethel?
How long did Jacob remain in Laban's house?
How did he fare? Did he **ever** return to Isaac?
By **whom was** he forgiven? Is it best to forgive? Matt. 5: 9. 6: 12. 18: 21, 22. Who forgives us? **Num.** 14: 20. Is. 44: 22. 55: 7. Matt. 9: 6.
What happened at Peniel?
What name was given to Jacob by **the angel?**
How did Jacob lose Joseph? Did **he ever** regain him?
To what land did aged Jacob go? Where was he when he **died?** How long did he live? By whom and **where** was he buried?

Notes. BIRTHRIGHT, the right of the eldest child, who received greater honor and a double portion of the inheritance. COMPELLED, insisted, urged, forced. MESS OF POTTAGE, a broth of beans, or lentils. GAME, wild creatures taken for food. DREAM, a vision during sleep. ANGELS, God's messengers. BLESSING, benefit. SERVED, worked for another. FORGIVEN, having the charge, **or** punishment for sins taken away. WRESTLED, struggled with. JEALOUSY, envy.

Lesson 9.—The Third Sunday in the Epiphany Season.

JOSEPH AND HIS BROTHERS. I.

COMMIT PROV. 10: 1, 2. READ GEN. 30: 22—37; 35.

THE STORY.

Israel's (Jacob's) 12 sons were Reuben, Simeon, Levi, Judah, Dan, Naphtali, Gad, Asher, Issachar, Zebulun, Joseph, Benjamin. All dwelt at Bethel and at Hebron in Canaan. Joseph was a noble boy. His father loved him best and gave him a fine coat. This made his brothers hate and scold him. But Joseph tried to be good and obey God and his father. In those days God often taught the people by means of dreams. When about 17 years old he dreamed that his brother's sheaves came and bowed to his sheaf in the field. He dreamed again that the sun, moon and eleven stars came and fell before his star. By these dreams the LORD showed that all his family, even his father should bow to Joseph. His brothers envied and persecuted him.
The older brothers being shepherds went away with their

flocks. Joseph was sent by his father to visit them far from home. They seized their young brother and cast him into a pit. It was only Reuben who persuaded the rest from killing him. While Reuben was absent the brothers sold Joseph to some passing children of Ishmael to carry him away and sell him for a slave. The wicked brothers took Joseph's coat, stained it with

Joseph sold by his Brothers.

the blood of a kid and went home to say that they found the robe with blood on it. So poor old Israel supposed that some lion had killed Joseph and mourned. How wicked is the sin of lying!

REVIEW.

Can you name Israel's sons in their order?
How many were they? Where did they dwell?
What do you remember about Bethel? Less. 8.
Tell the character of Joseph. How did his father therefore treat him?
Is our Heavenly Father pleased with good children? Eph. 5: 1. I. Peter 1: 14, 15.
How did the brothers treat Joseph? Why? I. Thess 4: 9. Gal. 5: 26.
Did this discourage Joseph in doing right? Gal. 6: 9. II. Tim. 4: 18. Jas. 1: 12.

Did God often use dreams in those days? Job 33: 15, 16. Gen. 28: 12. Acts 2: 16, 17.

What strange dreams did Joseph have? What did they mean?

What is envy? Do not the wicked always envy the good? Ps. 37: 12.

Is not contentment better than envy? Phil. 4: 12. James 3: 16. 9th and 10th Com.

What occupation had Joseph's brothers? What was Joseph sent to do? How did the brothers treat Joseph?

To whom was he sold? Less. 6 and 7.

What did the wicked brothers do with Joseph's coat?

Did they tell a lie? Is a lie a sin? 8. Com.

What did Israel suppose?

Who was sold like Joseph? Matt. 26: 14—16.

Notes. DWELT, lived. NOBLE, above what is mean or dishonorable. SHEAVES, bundles of grain in the field. TAUGHT, instructed. In our days having the Holy Bible as the full Word of God, we need not to be instructed by dreams. Hence God does not use them now. VISIT, to come as friend to friend to know his condition. SEIZED, caught hold of. SLAVE, one whose life and liberty have been bought, a servant without wages. ISHMAELITES, descendants of Ishmael, son of Abraham and Hagar. They dwelt in portions of Arabia and Syria. SUPPOSED, thought, imagined or believed. LYING, putting the false for the true.

Lesson 10.—The Fourth Sunday in the Epiphany Season.

JOSEPH AND HIS BROTHERS. II.

COMMIT Ps. 37: 5, 6. READ GEN. 37: 36—50.

THE STORY.

Joseph, the forsaken boy, was taken by the Ishmaelites to Egypt and again sold. He was bought by Potiphar, chief of the prison guard of Pharaoh the King.

Joseph did not forget what he had learned about God, but kept faithfully to his duty. The LORD blessed him. He was trusted and became Potiphar's steward. For Joseph's sake the LORD made his master rich. Potiphar had a vicious wicked wife, who tried to make Joseph sin against God and disgrace his master by committing the horrible crime of adultery.

He would do no such wickedness and sin against God. But he was unjustly accused and cast into prison. God gave him wisdom to explain the dreams of two prisoners,—the King's cup bearer and baker. Finding that Joseph had power (from

JOSEPH AND HIS BROTHERS. 23

God) to explain dreams, King Pharaoh himself sent for him to tell the meaning of two dreams of 7 fat and 7 thin cattle and 7 full and 7 wasted ears of corn. Joseph foretold 7 years of plenty and 7 years of famine in all Egypt. Then the King made him his chief officer and steward over the land. During the famine Joseph's brothers came down to Egypt starving and seek-

Joseph made Ruler.

ing to buy corn. Joseph saw them and helped them though they did not know him. When they went home with corn, he kept Simeon in Egypt till they should return bringing Benjamin his own younger brother with them. Israel was unwilling to allow this; but at last, through hunger he consented. On the second visit Joseph received them kindly and brought Simeon out to them.

Then, by pretending that Benjamin had taken his precious cup and hidden it in his sack of corn, he brought them back to his presence after a day's journey. They begged to have Benjamin forgiven. Then Joseph told them who he was, freely forgave them and invited all to come down to Egypt. He kept their families (70 souls) safely during the famine in Egypt. And

The Recognition.

Jacob saw Joseph once more. Thus God brought good out of evil, and thus Joseph's dreams were true. Joseph lived 110 years and his sons Ephraim and Manasseh were honored by each having a family portion equal to that of one of the sons of Israel. Jacob having adopted them as his own in place of Joseph who served Pharaoh.

REVIEW.

Into what land was Joseph carried? Who bought him?
Why did the LORD bless Joseph? Rev. 2: 10.
What is a steward? I. Cor. 4: 2. Luke 12: 42, 43.
Was Potiphar's wife a good person? What commandment was Joseph tempted to break? Against Whom would he have sinned?
Is Adultery a great wickedness? Lev. 20: 10.
Are the innocent sometimes unjustly punished?
How was Joseph punished? But does God forget those who try to be good and do right? Matt 5: 3—11.
What did Joseph do in the prison?
Who afterward sent for him?
What were Pharaoh's dreams and what did Joseph foretell?
What did Pharaoh make Joseph to be?
Who came to Egypt during the famine? Did Joseph help them? Matt. 5: 44, 45.
Relate what treatment they received from him.
What favor did Joseph do for his family? 4th Com.
What did Joseph show? Matt. 18: 21, 22. Rom. 12: 19—21.
By saving Egypt and his own family and forgiving them of Whom is he a type? Luke 23: 34.
Can God bring good out of the evil of men? Gen. 50: 20.
How did Jacob honor the sons of Joseph?

Notes. FORSAKEN, neglected, outcast. VICIOUS, full of bad ways. DISGRACE, dishonor, shame. CRIME, that which is against law ADULTERY, impure affection for the husband or wife of another. ACCUSED, charged. EXPLAIN, show clearly. STARVING, dying from hunger. PRETENDING, making believe that what is false is true. PRECIOUS, valuable, much thought of. HONORED, respected. FAMILY PORTION, a share of the inheritance.

Lesson 11.—The Fifth Sunday in the Epiphany Season.

JOB.

COMMIT 1. PETER 5: 6, 7. READ JOB CHAPT. 1, 2, 42.

THE STORY.

There lived long ago, a noble good man, named Job, as true and upright as he could be. He feared, loved and trusted in God above all things. He did not want to do any wrong thing. The LORD made him very rich and great.

In order to prove how strong Job's faith was the LORD allowed Satan to take away his oxen, asses, sheep, camels, his servants and even his ten children. Job only said "The LORD gave and the LORD hath taken away; blessed be the name of the LORD." He did not murmur nor charge God foolishly.

Satan was then permitted to afflict Job with sore boils from head to foot. Job in his misery sat down among the ashes. Then even his own wife told him to "curse God and die." This he would not do. Once he said: "Though He slay me yet will I trust in Him."

Job.

The friends of Job came to comfort him, but they only made his grief the greater by saying that God sent such sorrows in judgment of a man's wickedness, presumption and impatience. Of all these Job had not been guilty.

But Elihu, another friend, came to show that when Job thought only of his own goodness and praised himself he was wrong. This was not true piety nor religion. He justified *himself* rather than God. Then Job humbled himself very penitently before God. And the LORD spoke unto Job and showed His righteousness, power and wisdom. Job prayed also for his friends and while so doing, the LORD took away his sores. Job received twice as much wealth as before. All his friends came and offered comforts and gifts. God gave to patient Job seven more sons and the three fairest daughters in all the land. Then patient Job lived, amid peace and prosperity, so long that he saw his children's grandchildren.

REVIEW.

Tell me what kind of man Job was. Is it right to fear God? Deut. 5: 29. Ps. 111: 10. Eccles. 12: 13. Matt. 10: 28. Rom. 11: 20. Expl. of 1st Com.
How did he show his fear and love of God? Did God bless him? In what ways?
Did Satan trouble him? How? Why? What did Job say?
What bodily affliction befell Job? What did his own wife urge him to do? Did he yield to the temptation to murmur against God? Who came to comfort Job?
How did Elihu show Job his mistake? Job. 33: 2—5. Is self-righteousness piety? Is pride religion? What was Job's mistake?
When Job saw his error what did he do? Did the LORD help him? Is penitence a duty in every one? For whom did Job also pray? How did God exalt the patient penitent Job? Luke 14: 11.
How did God again bless him? When did He remove his affliction? Was Job's life after his affliction was ended long and peaceful? Ps. 37: 37. John 13: 7.

Notes. TRUE, honest, pure in heart. GREAT, honorable, respectable, distinguished. BLESSED, happy and praised. CHARGE, to lay blame upon. AFFLICT, to bring sorrow or trouble upon one. MISERY, wretchedness. CURSE, to ask that harm or trouble may fall upon any one. SLAY, kill. COMFORT, cheer, encourage. [God allows trouble not to make us murmur but to keep us lowly.] GRIEF, sorrow, despair. JUDGMENT, decision. PRESUMPTION, taking more honor than we should, forwardness. IMPATIENCE, a lack of contentment, uneasiness, fretting. PIETY, fear and reverence for God. RELIGION, union with God. JUSTIFIED, called himself right or good. PENITENTLY, sorrowfully and humbly. WEALTH, riches. PROSPERITY, plenty and success.

Lesson 12.—The Sixth Sunday in the Epiphany Season.

A LESSON IN REVIEW.

COMM. Ps. 145: 8, 9, 10. READ HEBREWS 11: 1—22.

THE STORY.

Our first lesson told us how God in six days created the Heavens and the Earth. Then, on the seventh day He rested;

thus making it the first Sabbath or holy day. Adam and Eve, our first parents, lived in innocence in a beautiful Garden, "Eden." Then we read how they disobeyed God and fell into sin. They were driven from Eden. Cain, the first son jealously killed his loving brother Abel. Seth was the third son of Adam. Enoch walked with God and was not found, for God took him. The Flood destroyed the wicked world, but God saved faithful Noah in the Ark, with his family and two of every creature.

Wicked men tried to build a Tower of safety. God changed and mixed their language, separated them and made their work confusion.

Faithful Abraham in Canaan saved Lot, established circumcision, sent away Hagar and Ishmael and reared peaceful Isaac, the "child of promise." Isaac's twin sons were Esau and Jacob. Jacob, after his 20 years of toil, led his family home to Canaan and became Israel, the father of the Jews. Noble Joseph, the beloved of his father Israel, though forsaken by his eleven brothers, forgave and saved them and their little ones. Job, pious, upright and rich; though afflicted and bereaved, was at first self-righteous, but patient, then penitent, and, at last, blessed by the LORD who is "true to all."

REVIEW.

Who made heaven and earth? Gen. 1: 1. Ps. 124: 8.
Can you give the order of the Creation? Less. 1.
How did the seventh day become the Sabbath?
How did the first people live? What were their names?
What became of them? Who was Cain?
What wickedness did he do? What became of Enoch? Why?
How did God destroy the wicked world? Who were saved? How?
Should we fear another flood? Less. 4.
What did other wicked men try to build?
How did the LORD check them?
Tell of Abraham. Whom did he save? What covenant did he establish? Whom did he send away?
What title was given to Isaac? Of whom was he the father?
Who was Jacob? To what land did he bring his family?
What name did God give him? What great nation is descended from him? Which of his sons was the noblest?
Can you tell the story of Joseph? How many brothers had Joseph?
Who was Job? What great virtues did he show?
Did God bring him through all his afflictions and sorrow?
Will the LORD ever be faithful to all?
How has He shown that faithfulness? Acts 3: 25, 26.

Lesson 13.—Septuagesima Sunday.

MOSES AND AARON.

Commit Ps. 77: 19, 20. Read Exodus, Leviticus, Numbers and Deuteronomy.

THE STORY.

The Israelites remained in Egypt 216 years. In Levi's tribe Miriam, Aaron and Moses were born. Pharaoh and the Egyptians hated the Israelites, because they grew to be so many. The king made the Israelites slaves and even ordered all the new

Moses saved.

born boys to be cast into the River Nile. When Moses was born his mother kept him safely hidden, three months. When she could no longer keep him she laid her beautiful babe in a little ark, or boat, among the reeds that grew in the river. Miriam, the older child, was left near by to watch her little brother.

Pharaoh's daughter came by, found the little ark and adopted Moses. She sent Miriam and employed the mother to come, take away and nurse this child for her. He grew up in the king's palace.

When Moses became 40 years of age, he slew an Egyptian who was beating an Israelite slave. For this he fled and lived for 40 years a shepherd in the land of Midian.

When he was eighty years old, the LORD appeared to him as a light, burning in a bush. He bade him go to Egypt—find Aaron his brother, and with Aaron to lead all the Israelites out of Egypt. He obeyed, went to Egypt, told Pharaoh what God's will was and when the King hardened his heart, Moses did many miracles, with God's help, among which were the "ten plagues:" i. e. the River was turned to blood; frogs, lice, flies were brought, disease destroyed the cattle, boils came upon the people, hail, locusts and thick darkness fell upon the land; and at last the first-born of every house in Egypt died. When at length Pharaoh did let the Hebrews, (Israelites) go, he followed with his army to try to bring them back to be his slaves again. But God was with them. He sent a Cloud, which was dark by day and bright by night, so as to guide and defend them. God made a path for them through the Red Sea and Moses led them to the other side safely. But the Egyptians following were drowned in the Sea. Wherever the LORD's cloud went, Moses led the people; He was called to go up to the top of Mt. Sinai, to meet the LORD; who appeared in a thick cloud amid thunderings and lightnings. He received there the "Ten Commandments;" written by the finger of God upon two tablets of stone. Moses is called thus the Law-giver. He wrote the first five books of the Bible, the Pen-ta-teuch. Aaron, who aided his brother Moses, became High Priest of Israel. The High Priest is a type of Jesus the "Great High Priest" because he offered sacrifice and prayed for the people.

REVIEW.

How long did the descendants of Jacob (Israel) remain in Egypt?
Who were born in Levi's tribe?
Did the Egyptians love the children of Israel?
How did Pharaoh show his dislike to them?
Who saved the baby Moses? How did she do it?

Who found the child? What became of the child?
For what did Moses flee from Egypt?
What did he do in the Land of Midian?
Did the LORD appear to him there? How?
What did the LORD command? Did he obey?
What were the ten plagues? See Exodus 7 to 12.

Moses and the Children of Israel across the Red Sea.

Why did Pharaoh follow the Israelites?
How did God help Israel? Did Pharaoh safely cross the sea?
How did Moses know where to lead Israel?
To meet the LORD, what mountain did Moses ascend?
Did God give him anything there?
Can you recite the Ten Commandments?

What title does Moses sometimes receive?
Did Moses write any part of the Bible?
What office did Aaron fill?
Of Whom does his office remind us? What were his chief duties?
Hebrews 5: 1—5, 8—10.

Moses receiving the Ten Commandments.

Notes. TRIBE, one family of a great nation. CAST, thrown. EMPLOYED, hired, engaged for labor. PALACE, a grand house. FLED, ran quietly away. BADE, commanded. MIRACLES, Gods works done above the usual ways of nature. PLAGUES calamities, wide spread evils. HEBREWS, the descendants of Heber. [See Gen. 11: 15—17; 14: 13] GUIDE, to lead. DEFEND, to protect from harm. TABLETS, plates, slabs. AIDED, helped. HIGH PRIEST, the head or the chief of the priestly family. SEPTUAGESIMA, the Latin word 70, to show that Easter comes seventy days later.

Lesson 14.—Sexagesima Sunday
MOSES AND AARON. II.
COMMIT ISAIAH 55: 4. READ EXODUS, NUMBERS, LEVITICUS, DEUTERONOMY.

THE STORY.

Upon the night, when all the first-born of the Egyptians died, the children of Israel had marked their doors with the blood of a lamb. Each family gathered and ate the lamb as if

Moses breaking the tablets of the Commandments.

ready to start for a long journey. While they were doing this, the punishing angel of death *passed over* their marked houses.

This was the first time that the "Passover" was celebrated. It became an annual festival of liberty and took place at our time of Easter. The Passover Lamb is an emblem of Christ Jesus.

While Moses was with God upon Mt. Sinai, Israel sinned by persuading Aaron to make a calf of gold, such as the Egyptians worshiped. When Moses came down from the mountain, he saw the people leaping and dancing, worshiping the idol calf. In his

The Spies returning.

sorrow he threw down and broke the stone tablets of the commandments.

Moses ground the calf to powder and scattered it upon the water; and obtained from God another copy of the Law. Moses led Israel by following the Cloud of the LORD through the wilderness. "Manna" was sent down from heaven for the people to gather daily to eat, and God opened in a rock a fountain of water to flow after them in the desert. The LORD defended them from their enemies and rebuked the sedition of Aaron and Miriam. Moses sent out twelve spies to view the "Land of Promise." Ten

The brazen Serpent.

of them brought back an ill report of the country. Then the people murmured. So God sent the people back to wander in the wilderness forty years, till all who had started from Egypt were dead save the two good spies.

A mutiny by Korah and others was stopped. The LORD opened the earth and it swallowed up Korah and his men.

Twelve rods of the tribes were laid before the LORD. Aaron's rod began to bud and brought forth almonds. It was kept as a memorial of God's displeasure with rebels and the choice of Aaron to be His Priest. At a place where poisonous serpents bit them, Moses put a brass figure of a serpent upon a pole, and all the bitten ones who looked upon it were healed.

At the end of Moses' life he blessed the tribes and went to Pisgah at the top of Mt. Nebo to view the land of Canaan. There, alone with God, he died, and the angels of God buried him. He lived 120 years. When Jesus was transfigured as the Son of God, Moses appeared with Elijah. Moses was meek dignified and faithful. He was a *Leader* and Deliverer. He reminds us of Christ, the Captain of our Salvation, and the perfect Example of law fulfilled.

REVIEW.

How had the Israelites marked their doors on the night of the death of the first born in Egypt?
What was each family doing?
What is this event now called? Why?
When is it kept?
Of Whom is the Easter-lamb a type? Is. 53: 7. John 1: 29. Heb. 9: 28. I. Peter 2: 24.
How did Aaron and Israel sin?
What did Moses see?
What did he do with the idol?
What happened to the tablets of Commandments?
Did Moses get another copy of the Law? Exod. 34: 1—4, 27—29.
Which commandment had Israel broken? James 2: 10.
How long were the Israelites wandering? Why?
How do we know that God took care of them?
Does he care for us? Matt. 6: 30.
How were the Israelites defended and preserved? Ps. 78: 15, 20.
Whom did Moses send into Canaan?
For what purpose?
How did they report?
What was the effect of this?
How was Korah's rebellion put down?
Tell something about Aaron's rod.
How was Israel saved from the bites of fiery serpents?
Did those who looked believe in God?
Who was lifted up to save us? John 3: 14, 15.
Where did Moses end his life? How?
Has Moses ever reappeared? Matt. 17 3. **When?**
What does this show about life after death?

Tell what you know about Moses' character?
How does Moses remind us of our Saviour? Heb. 2: 10, 11. I. Peter 2: 21.
Who is compared to the Rock that supplied water to Israel? I. Cor. 10: 4.

Notes. PASSOVER, the passing over and sparing of the Israelites by the angel when the Egyptians were destroyed, causing the liberty of Israel. EASTER, the Christian's festival of the Passover, teaching the resurrection of the dead. WORSHIP, to honor and admire as a God. IDOL, a figure or picture of God, made for worship. MANNA, ("What is this?") a strange food sent from God and found each morning, except the Sabbath, round the camp of Israel. SEDITION, a quarrel and separation in a nation. CANAAN, the beautiful land between Syria and Egypt, promised to Abraham, Isaac, Jacob and to the children of Israel. It belonged at first to the descendants of Canaan (See Gen. 10: 15—20), but was doubtless taken from them on account of their wickedness. SAVED, set free from harm. TRANSFIGURED, changed in appearance. SEXAGESIMA, (sixtieth), this Sunday is so called because it is now sixty and three days before Easter.

Lesson 15.—Quinquagesima Sunday.

THE TABERNACLE.

COMMIT II. CORINTHIANS 5: 1. READ EXODUS 25 TO 31.

THE STORY.

When the LORD came down to Moses on Mt. Sinai, He showed him how he should make for the people a moveable Church, or TABERNACLE. The *Levites* were to have charge of it and set it up like a large tent every time that Israel encamped. A space 1800 by 900 feet, was called the "Court" and enclosed by *Curtains* hanging between *Pillars*. The *Gate* was toward the East.

Near the Gate, within, stood a large brazen *Altar* for sacrifices, in which fire was kept continually burning. Beyond it stood the *Laver*, a large vessel of water for purifying and washing. In the midst of the Court stood the *Tabernacle* itself, facing eastward. It contained two rooms, the first twice as long as the second. These were separated by a beautiful linen *Curtain*, embroidered with blue, purple, and scarlet in patterns of angels. Four coverings were put over the Tabernacle.

The larger room of the Tabernacle was called "The Holy Place." It contained in the centre an *Altar of Incense*, where prayer to God was daily made. On the North side stood a *Table of Shewbread*; having 12 loaves of bread, new each week, placed by the priests. On the South side stood a *Golden Candlestick*, or lampstand, having 7 branches and lights.

The "Most Holy Place," (or "Holy of Holies,") beyond the "Vail," (or Curtain) kept, in solemn silence, the golden *Ark of the Covenant*; a precious Chest, holding the *Ten Commandments*, written on the two tables of stone; a golden vessel of *Manna* and *Aaron's Rod* that budded.

The Lid of this Ark was called "The Mercy Seat." On each end of it was a golden angel, or *Cherub*.—Between the

Form and arrangement of the Tabernacle, Camp, etc.

Cherubs the LORD, in mercy, showed His presence by a *Light*, ("Shekinah").

The *Priests* only, (Aaron's family of Levites,) went into and took care of the *Holy Place*. The other Levites assisted them in sacrifices in the *Court*. The *High Priest* wore a *Mitre*, or beautiful cap; a *Robe* of fine linen, with bells and golden balls hanging alternately from its border; an *Ephod*, or fine coat, having a precious stone on each shoulder; a *Girdle;* and a *Breastplate*, composed of twelve stones set in gold.

No one, save the High Priest, dared to enter the Holy of Holies, and he only once a year; on the great "Day of Atonement;" when he came before that Light of the merciful God, to pray for the forgiveness of all the people.

REVIEW.

While on Mt. Sinai what was Moses commanded to make?
Why was it moveable?
For whose blessing was the Church built?
Who had charge of it?
How large was the Court?
What stood in it? Where was the Gate?

Ark of the Covenant.

How many rooms were in the Tabernacle?
Were they of equal size?
How were these rooms separated?
What covered the Tabernacle?
By what name was the larger room known?
Can you tell what was in that room?
Tell the name of the small room?
What was solemnly kept there?
What did that Ark contain? See Heb. 9: 2—7.
What was the Lid of the Ark called?
Who appeared between the Cherubim? Why?
Of Whom is the light a likeness? Acts 2: 3.
What were the Priests' duties?
Could they enter the Tabernacle?

Who were the Priests?   Who were the Levites?
What was their duty?
Describe the dress of the High Priest.
Did he dare to enter the Holy of Holies?   How often?
On what day?
Why did he come before God?

Notes. TABERNACLE (a tent). This moveable Temple was about 18 feet high, 18 feet wide and 54 feet long: built by placing upright gilded boards each 18 feet high and 30 inches wide; locking them together by five bars on each side run through rings of gold set into the boards. ENCLOSED, shut in. (The teacher will explain, if possible, how large such a field or area would be.) PILLARS, columns. COURT, the space around a building. BRAZEN, made of copper or brass. CONTINUALLY, always. PURIFYING, making clean. EMBROIDERED, ornamented with needlework. COVERINGS, the first, or inner covering of the Tabernacle was fine linen, like the curtain; the second was of woven goats' hair, the third of rams' skins, dyed red; and the fourth of badgers' skins. INCENSE, Substances, which are burned to make a sweet perfume before the LORD. HOLY PLACE, the dimensions of the Holy Place were probably 18 feet wide, 18 feet high and 36 feet long: the Most Holy Place was 18 feet each way. SOLEMN, sacred, awe-inspiring. "SHEKINAH, the light of the glory of God, by which the people knew the presence of God. (See Matt. 17: 5. Luke 2: 9.) ASSISTED, aided, helped. MITRE, a high cap on which was written "Holiness to the LORD." ROBE, a garment for the body. GIRDLE, a belt, or sash. BREASTPLATE, this beautiful plate contained 12 stones in four rows of three; each inscribed with a name of a tribe of Israel, the following is supposed to be the order; 1. Sardius (or Carnelian of Sardis). 2. Topaz (our Chrysolite of greenish yellow). 3. Carbuncle (our Emerald, green [probably]). 1. Emerald (interchanged with Carbuncle, red). 2. Sapphire.3. Diamond (supposed to be the onyx, alabaster or jasper). 1. Ligure, (or jacinth, blue). 2. Agate.3. Amethyst (purple). 1. Beryl.2. Onyx (lined black and white). 3. Jasper (dark green). ATONEMENT, reconciliation, or bringing to one mind those at strife. MERCIFUL, full of pity and help. FORGIVENESS, the taking away of guilt and punishment. QUINQUAGESIMA, (fiftieth) a name applied to this Sunday because it is now fifty and six days until Easter. ASH WEDNESDAY, during the following week, begins the season called Lent.

Lesson 16.—The First Sunday in Lent.

JOSHUA.

COMMIT HEBREWS 13: 14.   READ THE BOOK OF JOSHUA.

THE STORY.

One of the Hebrew slaves, (Israelites, Jews) who started with Moses and Aaron from Egypt, was Joshua of the tribe of Ephraim; a brave, wise man, full of faith in the LORD and of willingness to obey Him. While Moses kept praying for the people, (his hands being upheld by Aaron and Hur) Joshua, the general over Israel, drove away the Amalekites. He became Moses' helper, or attendant, and part of the way went with him up Mt. Sinai. He was one of the 12 men sent by Moses to spy out Canaan. Ten of these reported the land to be very bounti-

JOSHUA.

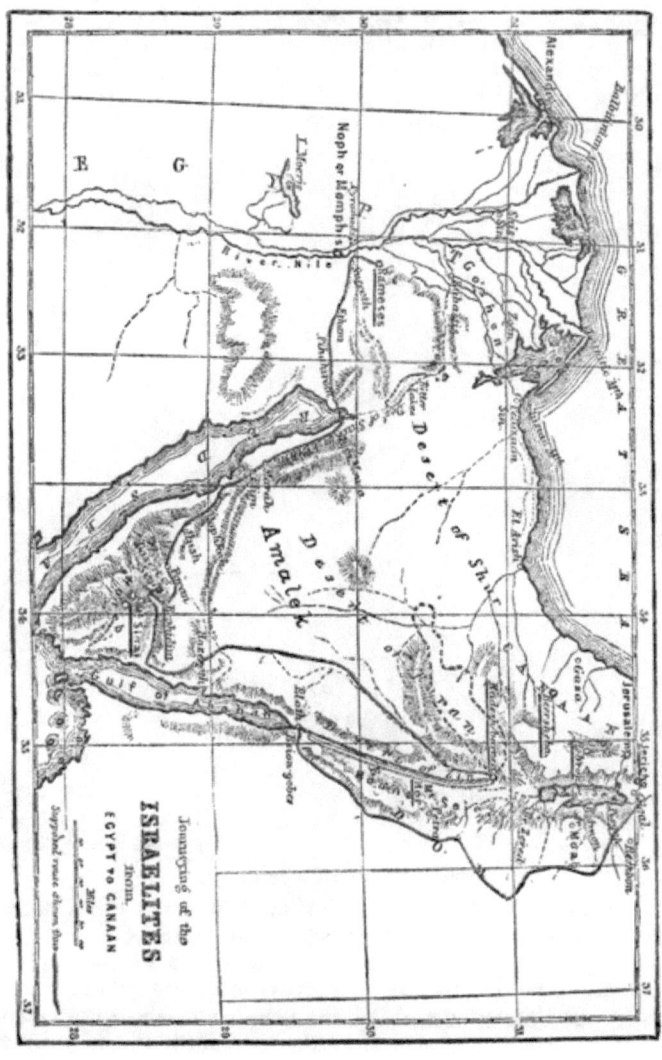

ful, but that giants dwelt there, and the Israelites being strangers could not get the land. But Joshua and Caleb, the other spies, told all to "go forward" trusting that God would give them "the land flowing with milk and honey." Israel murmured, feared and would not go on. Hence the LORD turned them back into

Israel entering the city of Jericho.

the wilderness, to wander about for forty years, till all were dead who had started from Egypt, save Joshua and Caleb.

At Moses' death Joshua took the command as Leader, as God had said. He led the people across the river Jordan; while God kept back the water and lo! the people stood in the "Land of Promise." Joshua now renewed the covenant of the people with God, by circumcising all those who were uncircumcised. At Jericho the people marched seven days around the city. Then the Priests blew their trumpets and Israel gave a shout, when God caused the gates and walls to fall, so that Joshua's men easily took the city and destroyed it. One by one, other wicked cities were taken. At Gibeon, the LORD permitted Joshua to command the Sun and Moon to stand still, so that a great victory could be won. Joshua now, by lot, divided the whole land among all the tribes, except that of Levi, but gave that of Joseph two shares, one for Ephraim the other for Manasseh. The Levites were allowed to live in 48 cities among all the other tribes, because they were the sacred, or priestly tribe. Joshua then set up the Tabernacle to abide at Shiloh, and appointed six cities of Refuge, for justice. After once more renewing the covenant between the LORD and Israel, Joshua, the servant of God, died, aged 110 years. As Joshua led, renewed and saved Israel, so has CHRIST led His Church through death, renewed it by resurrection, and saved it forever in Heaven.

REVIEW.

Who was Joshua? Which was his Tribe? How was he a good man? What office did he fill?

As Moses prayed, what did Joshua do?

Is God pleased with prayer?

Does He wish us to pray?

What kind of a heart does prayer show?

Is prayer answered?

How did Joshua help Moses? Exod. 24: 12, 13.

What is a spy?

How did Joshua prove faithful as a spy? Num. 13: 8. 14: 6—10.

Would Israel take the advice he gave? Num. 14: 10.

How therefore did the LORD punish Israel? Num. 14: 30.

After Moses' death who led Israel? Deut. 31: 23. Joshua 1: 1, 2.

How did Israel cross the river Jordan?

What covenant was renewed?

How was Jericho overcome?

What great miracle occurred at Gibeon? Joshua 10: 13.

Can you tell how Joshua divided the land?

For what were six cities of Refuge set apart?

Where was the Tabernacle finally set up?

What last act did Joshua perform?

Whose servant was Joshua?

How old was Joshua at his death?

What may we learn of Christ from the life of Joshua?

THE JUDGES.

Notes. LENT, ("lengthening,") the 46 Spring-days before Easter set to commemorate the sufferings of Christ. UPHELD, kept up in place. ATTENDANT, one who assists, or serves another. SPY, to look, or examine secretly. MURMURED, complained against God. COMMAND, authority to control others. LEADER, one who conducts, or guides. COVENANT, the promise of God to bless the faithful. CAUSED, made. REFUGE, a retreat, a place of safety. The six cities of Refuge: Kedesh, Shechem, Hebron, Bezer, Ramoth, Golan: (3 on either side of the Jordan,) were places to which those fled for safety and a fair trial, who were charged with any crime. RESURRECTION, rising from the dead.

Lesson 17.—The Second Sunday in Lent.

THE JUDGES.

COMMIT ROMANS 2: 14—16. READ THE BOOK OF JUDGES.

THE STORY.

No leader arose when Joshua died. The people began to forget God and serve idols. Then they could not drive away all their enemies. And God sent an angel to reprove them. Judges now ruled and led the tribes of the people to war. Great Princes, such as Chushan, Eglon and Sisera attacked Israel; and Othniel, (Caleb's nephew) Ehud, Shamgar and Barak defeated these enemies. Deborah, a prophetess aided the hero Barak, and Jael slew the fleeing Sisera who hid in her tent. Thus Israel drove away the Philistines.

Gideon, whom an angel of God called to duty, broke down the idol-altar before his father's house and called to all Israel to follow him against the Midianites, who now oppressed them. Signs of God's help were given to Gideon. A fleece of wool was placed on the ground, and, during the night, the dew only fell on that fleece. The next night the fleece was dry, while much dew rested on all the ground. 32,000 men followed Gideon's call. But this army was, at God's command, reduced to 300. To show that it was God alone who could conquer the enemy, Gideon's little band were given lamps, pitchers and trumpets only. They formed a circle round the enemy's great camp, by night, hiding their lights in their pitchers. At Gideon's cry they threw down their pitchers, held up their lights and blew their trumpets. The Midianites awaking frightened fought and slew each other, or fled in great panic; Gideon then ruled in peace. Abimelech, his son, was very wicked, and was slain by his people.

THE JUDGES. 45

Tola, Jair, Jephtha (who made a rash vow and lost his daughter), Ibzan, Elon, Abdon, each judged Israel.

Gideon.

One day an angel appeared to Manoah and his wife, telling them that they should have a son. When born he was named

46 THE JUDGES.

Samson, became the strongest of men and did many feats of power. His wife was Delilah, a Philistine. He slew a lion with his own hands. He smote many Philistines. He burned the grain, by letting foxes that had firebrands tied to them run

Samson.

among the fields of the enemy. He carried away the great gates of the city of Gaza.

At last the Philistines found that the secret of his strength was in his long hair which had never been cut. They compelled his wife to cut off his hair, then made him a prisoner, put out his eyes and made him grind corn as a slave. On a great holiday,

THE JUDGES.   47

desiring sport, they brought blind Samson (whose hair had grown again), forth into a large company, to test his strength. The house rested mainly on two great columns. Finding these, Samson pulled both down together and the house fell, killing himself and all the people. He is the last Judge mentioned. The whole period of the Judges is about 300 years.

REVIEW.

Did a new Leader take Joshua's place when he died?
What great sin did the people begin to commit?   1st Com.
How did God show them their sin?
By whom were the tribes ruled and led?
Can you say who attacked the children of Israel?
And who defended them?
Who aided Barak?
Who killed Sisera?
An angel called a hero to duty; whom?
What did Gideon do?
How did the LORD show His care of Gideon?
How many men came at Gideon's call?
Was this army too large?
To what number was it reduced?
Did Gideon's band carry swords, spears and shields?
Tell what they had with them.
Can you describe the way the victory was won?
Name the Judges that followed after Gideon.
Who made a rash promise, or vow?
To whom did an angel appear?   What did he promise?
What was the name of the child?   What did he become?
Whom did he marry?
Can you mention any of his exploits?
What did the enemy find the secret of his strength to be?
How did the Philistines overcome him?
Desiring sport, what did they make him do?
What great destruction did he cause?
Does the judgment of the LORD rest upon evil doers?   Exod. 6: 6.
Who shall come at the last day to be our Judge?   Matt. 25: 32, 33.
Acts 17: 31.   Apos. Creed Art. II.

Notes. ENEMIES, those who fight each other. ANGEL, a heavenly spirit. JUDGES, those who administered justice. HERO, one who does noble things. PHILISTINES, idol worshipers who lived west of the land of Judah. MIDIANITES, a people in Arabia. REDUCED, made less. CONQUER, overpower. PANIC, fear, confusion and disorder. Vow, a solemn promise. RASH, not well considered, hasty FEATS, surprising actions. PERSUADED, induced. SPORT, pleasure. COLUMNS, pillars, usually supporting a roof or a building.

Lesson 18.—The Third Sunday in Lent.

RUTH.

COMMIT ST. MATT. 5: 4, 5. READ THE BOOK OF RUTH.

THE STORY.

While the Judges ruled Israel a great famine befell the land. Elimelech took Naomi, his wife with his two sons, and

Ruth.

leaving his own town of Bethlehem in the tribe of Judah, brought them into the land of Moab. There Chilion, one son, married

Orpah; Mahlon, the other, married Ruth. Their wives were maidens of Moab. But, alas! the father and both the sons died in Moab.

Noble, self-denying, helpless Naomi urged her two widowed daughters-in-law to go back to their own people. Orpah, thinking of her own comfort, did so. But self-denying Ruth followed poor, lonely Naomi, saying: "Intreat me not to leave thee;" "thy people shall be my people, and thy God my God." So Naomi brought Ruth with her to Bethlehem. They came during the barley harvest. Now Boaz, a rich and good kinsman of Elimelech, dwelt in Bethlehem. Ruth went out as a gleaner into the harvest-field, to gather a little of the grain that fell to the ground, not bound by the reapers. She happened to go into the field of Boaz. She was so modest, humble and industrious that she gained praise from all. A good report of her was even brought to Boaz, the master, when he came out to visit the field.

He became her friend, and rewarded her virtue and diligence by filling her mantle with grain. Afterward he acknowledged his kinship to poor Naomi; and, according to the Jewish law, bought Naomi's field and took Ruth, the poor Moabitess, to be his wife.

Boaz and Ruth were blessed by all for their piety and goodness of heart. God prospered them and they became the parents of Obed, the grand-father of David, King of Israel.

REVIEW.

What terrible affliction befell Israel in the days of the Judges?
Had this ever happened before? Lesson 10. Gen. 12: 10.
What did Elimelech do? Who went with him?
Into what land did they come?
How did the family fare in the land of Moab?
How did Naomi advise her daughters-in-law?
Was this noble? Why?
What did Orpah do?
What did Ruth say?
What kind of a spirit was this?
May we learn of faith in God from Ruth?
At what season did they come to Bethlehem?
Who lived at Bethlehem?
Was the famine past?
What did Ruth offer to do? Lev. 19: 9, 10.
Into whose field did she happen to go?
How did she conduct herself?

What did her behaviour gain for her?
Who heard of her?
Did he treat her kindly?
Did he bestow a gift upon her?
How did Boaz afterward fulfill the Jewish law? Leviticus 25: 25. Ruth 4: 6—10.

May even poor heathen people learn to believe in the true God and serve Him?
Is it better to be lowly than proud?
Is it better to be selfish or self-denying?
Why were Boaz and Ruth blessed by all?
Who prospered them?
What great man was descended from them?
Was not Jesus also descended from them? See Matt. 21: 9: Luke 3: 23, 31, 32.

Notes. RULED, commanded the people. SELF-DENYING, not pleasing oneself, living to bless others. URGED, tried to induce or persuade. HARVEST, the time of gathering the crop. (Barley harvest—was in March or April, according to locality.) KINSMAN, a relative. MODEST, not puffed up with pride. HUMBLE, lowly. INDUSTRIOUS, working with a will, not idling. VIRTUE, good character. MANTLE, a large wrap worn over the head and shoulders. ACKNOWLEDGED, knew and confessed.

Lesson 19.—The Fourth Sunday in Lent.

SAMUEL.

COMMIT PSALM 99: 6.   READ I. SAMUEL 1—25; 23: 3—25.

THE STORY.

After the death of Samson, the High Priest Eli remained the only ruler. In his days, pious Hannah praying came to the Tabernacle, lamenting that she had no child. Eli promised that her prayer should be answered and that the LORD would give her a son. She vowed to give him to the LORD for life. This precious child was named Samuel; or "asked from God." As soon as he was old enough, she brought him to Eli; to be his little servant in the Tabernacle at Shiloh. Eli's sons were bad and unfit to be Priests; but Samuel grew up to be good, wise and holy. One night, the LORD called twice to Samuel and twice Samuel went to Eli; saying, "Here am I, for thou didst call me." At last Eli knew that it was God Who spoke and, told Samuel, if the LORD called him once more, to say,—"Speak, LORD, for Thy servant heareth." The LORD called Samuel and said that old Eli and his sons would soon die. War began with the Philistines and Eli's impious sons even took the Ark of the Covenant out of the Tabernacle into the battle. But the wicked sons were killed, and the Ark was taken by the enemy to the temple of their idol. At the sad news old Eli died also.

But the LORD caused the idol of the Philistines to fall down and break in the temple before the Ark, and the people were

The child Samuel.

afflicted till they sent back the Ark to Israel. Samuel prayed. The LORD heard him and drove away the enemy. Samuel led in the conflict and set a stone of victory called Eben-e-zer, or "stone of help." Then Samuel became High Priest and ruler over all Israel.

But Samuel's sons were wicked too. The people rejected them as rulers, and came to Samuel, crying, "Give us a King!"

Samuel asked the LORD, Who said: "Make Saul a King." So Samuel anointed Saul to be the first King of Israel. Samuel urged all to be faithful, and even rebuked the King himself when he disobeyed God. He also anointed David to be King when Saul should die.

Samuel died in his old age. But God let Saul see a vision of Samuel, who appeared from the dead, to warn the wicked King that he would die the next day. Samuel was a Prophet.

REVIEW.

At Samson's death who was High Priest?
For what did a pious woman pray?
Did Eli promise that God would give her a son?
What was the mother's name?
Tell what "Samuel" means.
Does the Lord always fulfill his promises? Acts 2: 39.
Is it right to ask of God? John 16: 23, 24.
What vow did Hannah make?
To whom was Samuel brought?
Were Eli's sons good men?
How did Samuel grow up?
Does God know all? Prov. 15: 3.
Who spoke to Samuel by night?
What sad news came from God? 4th Com. Ps. 34: 15, 16.
What great loss befell Israel in war?
What became of the Ark?
How did this affect old Eli?
What happened among the Philistines, who kept the Ark?
How did Samuel show that Israel's help was in God, and not in man? James 5: 16,
Did God cause Samuel to succeed?
What two offices did Samuel fill?
Why did not Samuel's sons become Priests and Judges?
For what officer did the people cry?
How did Samuel ask counsel?
What did the LORD say?
Whom did Samuel anoint?
How did Samuel spend his life?
Whom did he afterward anoint as the next King?
Did Samuel ever appear after death? To whom?

Notes. LAMENTING, grieving, mourning. HOLY, pure in heart and life. AFFLICTED, vexed with suffering, or trouble. REJECTED, refused to accept, cast away. ANOINTED, appointed by the LORD to a holy office: (the Prophet pouring holy oil upon the head of the officer). REBUKED, chided, reproved. VISION, a supernatural sight. WARN, advise of danger, prepare the mind. PROPHET, a teacher, especially one whom the LORD inspires to see, know and tell the future. Acts 3: 24.

KING SAUL.

Lesson 20.—The Fifth Sunday in Lent.
KING SAUL.
Commit II. Samuel 1: 23, 24. Read I. Samuel 9—31.

THE STORY.

In the Tribe of Benjamin was Saul. He was noble, handsome, choice and head and shoulders taller than any other man

David and Goliath.

in Israel. Kish, his father, sent him to find some asses that went astray. Having lost his way, he found Samuel the prophet, who welcomed and anointed him as the future first King of Israel.

King Saul.

It came to pass as Samuel said. Saul was chosen King. The multitude shouted "God save the King," and laid many costly gifts at his feet. The brave Saul gathered soldiers and defended Israel. But the King was so impatient to conquer, that, instead

Saul and Jonathan.

of waiting for Samuel the High Priest to come, he took upon himself the Priest's duty of offering the sacrifice before the battle.

This was disobedience to God, and the LORD foretold that He would take away the Kingdom from the son of Saul and give it to another.

KING SAUL.

Both very brave Saul and Jonathan, his oldest son, won great praise for valor. But alas! Saul was sad-hearted and became gloomy and melancholy. In his day Goliath, a great Philistine giant, dared any man of Israel to battle with him! The boy David came to the camp of Israel and killed the giant. For this Saul was pleased with David and honored him, but afterward he envied, persecuted and tried to slay David.

Jealous Saul in a rage slew the Priests of the LORD because they befriended David. In Saul's despondency and fear, he forsook prayer and God, and went to ask advice of dead Samuel by a wicked witch, who pretended to bring the dead back to the living.

To their great terror, Samuel really appeared before the witch and Saul; told them of their sins, and said that Saul and his three sons should die on the morrow. This came to pass on Mount Gilboa the next day, in a battle against the Philistines. Saul was King for 40 years, and there was war during his reign.

REVIEW.

Can you describe young Saul? Of what Tribe was he?
Tell who was his father?
How did he help his father?
Whom did he meet while lost?
How did Samuel treat him?
Did Samuel promise anything?
Who was Samuel? What is a Prophet?
What is a Priest? What is a King?
[Can you tell how JESUS is a Prophet, Priest and King?]
What did the people do when Saul became King?
What did brave Saul do?
What wrong act did Saul perform?
Was it wrong for the King to pretend to be the Priest?
Had God anointed him to be a Priest, or a King?
What is a wrong act? James 4: 17.
How did the LORD punish Saul?
Does God know when we do wrong? II. Chron. 16: 9.
Who was Saul's oldest son?
What did Saul and his son gain?
How was Saul troubled?
What enemy lived in Saul's day?
What did he dare any man of Israel to do?
How did Saul act when David slew the giant?
At last how did Saul do wickedly?

What duty did he forsake?
Whose advice did he try to ask? How?
What did the witch pretend to do?
Did Samuel appear? Did he advise Saul?
Had he sad news for naughty Saul?
Did his words prove true?
How were they fulfilled?
How long was Saul King?
Was his reign peaceful?

Notes. HANDSOME, beautiful to see. CHOICE, precious, fit to be selected. ASTRAY wandering away. WELCOMED, received gladly. KING, the man who has the highest power in the land. DEFENDED, kept away the enemy. IMPATIENT, unwilling to wait, quick tempered, hasty. BRAVE, fearless. VALOR, strength in courage. MELANCHOLY, low spirits, despondency. GIANT, a very large, strong man. HONORED, praised and favored. ENVIED, mourned at another's prosperity. PERSECUTED, tormented, ill treated. RAGE, furious anger. PRIEST, one who prayed, praised and sacrificed to God. FORSOOK, turned away from. WITCH, a woman who claimed to have special unnatural power. TERROR, fear, fright.

Lesson 21.—The Sixth Sunday in Lent, called Palm Sunday.

KING DAVID.

COMMIT PS. 24: 7—10. READ I. SAMUEL 16, TO I. KINGS 2: 11.

THE STORY.

In the little town of Bethlehem, of the land of Judah, lived a shepherd boy named David. He was the great grandson of Boaz and Ruth, and the youngest of Jesse's eight sons. God loved David, for he was faithful. Samuel, the prophet, came to Jesse's house to anoint David to be the King after Saul. The boy carefully watched his sheep and learned to use his sling, so as to drive away and destroy the lions and the bears. He also played upon the harp. Indeed so well did he play, that even King Saul sent for him; in order, by his sweet music, to drive away his sadness. David was earnest in his trust in God and in zeal. David's older brothers went to the war with King Saul; and the boy was sent to visit them in the camp. Whilst with his brothers, he saw the great Philistine giant, Goliath, 12 feet high, daring any man of Saul's army to come out against him. David, though but a boy, having only his sling, no shield, no spear, went alone against him. But he said: "I come to thee in the

Name of the LORD of hosts." With the first stone from David's sling Goliath was slain. The Philistines feared and ran, while the army of Israel rose up and gained a great victory over them.

For this great act King Saul at first loved David, but afterward jealously persecuted him. Jonathan and David were

David sparing Saul's Life.

dear friends. Saul made Michal, his daughter, David's wife. David at length had to flee for his life to the city of Gath, of the Philistines, where he pretended to be insane. Next he lived in a cave and twice spared Saul's life. When King Saul and Jonathan were slain, David lamented much.

David was first made King of the Tribe of Judah only, and

King David.

then after 7½ years of all Israel over whom he reigned for 32½ years. He was a brave Ruler and won great victories.

He joyfully brought from Shiloh the Ark of the Covenant into the Tabernacle, which he set up in the "City of David," or Jerusalem, on Mount Zion; where he had driven out the wicked Jebusites; and built a castle and palace. David had been a man of blood and war, so the LORD forbade his building a holy Temple to Him in Jerusalem. He was "the great King," yet he was a great sinner. Nathan the prophet rebuked

An Eastern House-Top.

David for his evil deeds. But his sins were severely punished and he repented bitterly. His proudest and most handsome son, Absolom, was killed in war, while trying to take the kingdom from his father.

David had many brave soldiers. His reign lasted for forty years. It was foretold that Christ should come from the family of David; and King David loved to sing, to the music of his harp, the beautiful Psalms; (many of which he wrote;) concerning the Saviour Who was to come.

KING DAVID.

REVIEW.

Of what town and Tribe was David?
Who were his relatives?
Can you tell what work he did?
Do you remember any other who was a shepherd?
Was he industrious?

David and Nathan.

Why did God love him? Who anointed him?
To what position was he thus appointed of God?
What instrument and weapon could he use? 1. Sam. 16: 15—23. 17: 40.
Who sent for him? Why?
What became of David's brothers?
What is trust? What is zeal?

David went to camp and what great enemy did he see and hear?
How tall was Goliath?
Did David venture to battle with Goliath?
But in Whose name did he go?
Who was slain, Goliath or David?   Why?
How did Saul treat David?
Who became dear friends?
What must David do?
How did he **twice** show a noble spirit?
What did he become?
Did he build a city?   Where?
Can you tell what he brought into it?
Why could he **not** build a Temple to God?
Was he a sinner?
Does sin do us harm?   Rom. 7: 23, 24.
How was David punished for his sins?
How long did he reign?
Tell what Absolom tried to do?
Who was foretold to come from David's family?   Isaiah 9: 7. 11: 1.
Matt. 1: 1.   21: 9.   Luke 2: 4.   [Who is Christ?]
What did David write?
What did the old King love to do?

Notes. SHEPHERD, **one who tends** sheep. SLING, an ancient weapon for throwing stones. HARP, a stringed instrument of music. TRUST, faith, confidence, reliance. ZEAL, an earnest wish to do good. SHIELD, a soldier's protection, carried on the arm. SPEAR, a pointed pole, a dart for attacking. GATH, a chief city of the Philistines, on the borders of the land of Judah. PRETENDED, feigned. INSANE, weak, or unsound of mind. SINNER, a wrong doer. REPENTED, was very sorry and tried to do better. REIGNED, ruled as a King. FORETOLD, said beforehand. PSALMS, Hymns of the olden time sung to the music of the Harp etc. PALM SUNDAY, the day which teaches us of the final coming of Our Lord Jesus to Jerusalem, amid the waving of palms, and "Hosannas" of the people. PALM, a kind of tree, its branch an emblem of victory and joy.

Lesson 22.—Easter Sunday.

KING SOLOMON.

COMMIT ISAIAH 9: 6, 7.   READ I. KINGS 1—11.   I. CHRONICLES 29 TO II. CHRONICLES 9.

THE STORY.

Solomon was born when David his father was King. He was named Solomon because he would reign peacefully. From among his many sons, David, before he died, chose his son Solomon to be King after himself. He urged Solomon to be faithful to God.

KING SOLOMON.   61

He was crowned at eighteen years of age, and reigned for forty years.

At first he obeyed his good father, but, on account of his Egyptian heathen wife, he gradually allowed the worship of

Solomon's Judgment.

idols. Yet Solomon loved the LORD and prayed for wisdom, to lead and judge the people in the true way. The LORD was pleased with such a prayer and made him the wisest of all men. As Solomon had preferred wisdom to riches, or honor; God gave him vast riches and honor beside. He soon began to show his wisdom by great judgments and sayings; and he became widely famous and his kingdom very rich. In proof of his good judgment the following account is given. Two mothers came to the King; the one with a child that was dead, the other having a living babe in her arms. The one woman said: "We lived in one house, each with our child; and in the night the child of this woman died while she slept. In the dead of night, finding her babe lifeless, she arose, took my child, laid it in her bosom and placed her dead child by me. In the morning I found that it was not my own son which was in my bosom!" But the other said: "No, the living is my son and the dead is thy son." So each claimed the child. The King commanded that a sword be brought, the living child be divided and half be given to each mother. The one womon now cried out: "O King! give her the child, let it not be slain!" The other said "Divide it." Then the wise King told his servants to give the child to her that would save its life; for she was indeed its mother Was not that a wise decision? King Solomon and his men took the precious cedar wood, stones, iron, brass, silver and gold; gathered before by David, and for $7\frac{1}{2}$ years built a most beautiful Temple to the LORD, in the city of Jerusalem, dedicating it with prayer. Here the LORD renewed the old Covenant, by promising blessings to those who faithfully loved Him and kept His Commandments, and threatening sorrow to those who hated Him and disobeyed His holy Law.

Only a few enemies opposed Solomon and the kingdom spread and prospered. The King lived in a splendid palace and sat upon a high, gorgeous throne of ivory and gold.

Kings and Queens came from far off lands to wonder at his honor, glory, riches and wisdom.

But alas! when Solomon grew old he turned away his heart from God, and helped to serve idols. The LORD then foretold trouble in his son's reign.

Afterward, let us hope, the King repented, left this wickedness behind him and turned back, to love and serve the LORD.

Wise Solomon wrote some of the Psalms, and the Books of Proverbs, Ecclesiastes and Canticles (or Song of Solomon). At his death he was buried at Jerusalem. As he was peaceful, wise, sublime and glorious, Solomon is a type of JESUS, the "Prince of peace" and "Lord of lords."

KING SOLOMON.

REVIEW.

Who was king when Solomon was born?
Why was he named Solomon? I. Chron. 22: 9, 10.
Did David prefer his son Solomon to his other sons?
Can you mention any other son of David?
How did David urge Solomon to live?
How old was Solomon when he was made King?
How long did he rule?
For what did the boy-king ask the LORD?
But what great sin did he allow? 1st. Com.
On whose account was it?
Was the LORD pleased with the prayer of Solomon?
What did the LORD give to Solomon?
How did he show his great wisdom? See Kings 3: 19—28.
What came to Solomon along with wisdom?
Did Solomon build a great house?
Of what was it built?
For what purpose was it erected?
How was it dedicated to the LORD?
What is prayer? James 1: 5, 6. I. John 3: 22.
What was the Covenant which God renewed with Solomon?
Does this Covenant still teach us our duty to God?
What is that duty? Eccles. 12: 13.
But does God love the obedient because of their faithfulness or only for their works? Rev. 2: 10.
How did He bless Solomon?
Was his kingdom great?
Tell how he lived.
Which would you prefer, wisdom or riches? Prov. 4: 7.
Solomon committed a great sin; what was it?
What was foretold? What is repentance?
What parts of the Bible did wise Solomon write?
Where was he buried?
Is he a type of Jesus Christ? Why?

Notes. EASTER, the festival, commemorating our Lord Jesus' rising from the dead. SOLOMON, a name signifying "Peaceable." PEACE, rest of mind and outward prosperity. CROWNED, made a King, by having a royal diadem put on his head. EGYPTIAN, belonging to a land southwest of Canaan or Judea. (See Map.) HEATHEN, one who does not know, or love the true God. GRADUALLY, step by step. ALLOWED, permitted. PRAYED, asked of God. WISDOM, understanding, judgment. PREFERRED, chose. RICHES, wealth. HONOR, love, praise, fame, admiration. DEDICATING, offering for a holy use. RENEWED, made new or fresh again. OPPOSED, tried to stop. THRONE, a royal and costly chair. WONDER, admire. SUBLIME, grand, noble hearted.

Lesson 23.—The First Sunday after Easter.
THE LATER KINGS.

Commit Ps. 24: 9, 10. Read I. Kings 11: 26 to II. Chronicles 36.

CHRONOLOGICAL TABLE.

B. C. 975. Rehoboam becomes King, and ten tribes revolt.

Kings of Judah, (and Benjamin.)	Kings of Israel, ("Ten Tribes.")
B. C.	B. C.
975—958. Rehoboam,	975—955. Jeroboam.
958—955. Abijah.	955—953. Nadab.†
955—914. Asa.	953—929. Baasha.
914—889. Jehoshaphat.	929—927. Elah.†
889—885. Jehoram.	927. Zimri.†
885—884. Ahaziah.†	927—918. Omri.
884—878. Athaliah (Qu).†	918—896. Ahab.†
878—839. Joash.†	896. Ahaziah.
839—810. Amaziah.†	896—884. Jehoram.†
810—758. Uzziah.	884—857. Jehu.
758—742. Jotham.	857—840. Jehoahaz.
742—726. Ahaz.	840—825. Joash.
726—698. Hezekiah.	825—784. Jeroboam II.
698—643. Manasseh.	784—773. (Anarchy.)
643—641. Amon.†	773. Zachariah.†
641—609. Josiah.†	773. Shallum.†
609 Jehoahaz.	773—763. Menahem.
609—599. Jehoiakim.	763—761. Pekahiah.†
606. Captivity in Babylon began.	761—739. Pekah.†
	739—730. (Confusion.)
599. Jehoiachin.	730—721. Hoshea.
599—588. Zedekiah.	721. The Captivity of the "ten Tribes" begins in Assyria.
588. Kingdom of Judah destroyed.	
536. Return of Judah from Babylon.	

Note. Those marked † were slain.

THE STORY.

Solomon's son, Rehoboam, was cruel. So ten tribes rebelled and chose for their King Jeroboam an idolater. From this time there were two kingdoms until the "Ten Tribes" were carried away. The other kingdom of "Judah" (and Benjamin) remained 133 years longer. Every King of "Israel" was an idolater, and very wicked. Their evil acts punished them in many ways.

THE LATER KINGS. 65

Some were lepers, some were slain. Twice there was no King. Thus the LORD permitted the evil to destroy itself.

Shalmanezer, King of Assyria, came and took the kingdom of Israel from Hoshea and carried the nation away, never to re-

Naaman healed.

turn; for the people were scattered. Hence they are often called the "Ten lost Tribes" of Israel. Strangers took their land.

The kingdom of Judah had many pious Rulers. Asa destroyed all idols, Jehoshaphat was a good man and a brave soldier. In his days the prophets Elijah and Elisha lived, and Elisha by power from God cured Naaman, the Syrian general, of leprosy, telling him to wash seven times in the river Jordan. Joash was at first good, then evil. Amaziah was a worthy King. Uzziah was a leper, but he also did right. Jonathan too was faithful to the LORD. Hezekiah was a noble King, and defended Judah, when Shalmanezer carried Israel away. Josiah repaired the Temple, read the Law of the LORD, destroyed idolatry and kept the solemn Passover. Manasseh, an evil King, reigned longest. The later Kings of Judah were wicked men. At length, Nebuchadnezzar, King of Babylon came, took Jerusalem and carried captive to Babylon, the whole kingdom of Judah. Here the sorrowing people remained in bondage for seventy years. Then they were permitted by noble King Cyrus and others penitently to return under various leaders. Under Ezra and Nehemiah, (B. C. 455) the people rebuilt Jerusalem and the Temple. They remained in Judea and Galilee, and were subject to their own, or foreign princes till the coming of the Saviour; and even to the destruction of Jerusalem by the Roman general Titus. (A. D. 70.)

REVIEW.

How was Rehoboam related to David?
Under what King did ten Tribes revolt? And why?
Had this been foretold? Less. 22. I. Kings 11: 11—13.
By what names were the two kingdoms known?
Who was the first King of the "Ten Tribes" or Israel?
Did he worship the LORD? Matt. 4: 10.
Which kingdom continued the longer, Israel or Judah?
How much longer?
What may we say of every king of Israel?
Does evil punish itself?
Mention how their sins were punished? Job 4: 8. Isaiah 57: 20. Ezekiel 18: 4.
How was the kingdom of Israel destroyed? By whom?
What is that nation often called? Who took the land?
Into what land were the "Ten Tribes" carried?
Had Judah any pious Kings? Mention some.
Two great prophets lived during the reign of Jehoshaphat, who were they?
Who was Naaman? How was he cured of his leprosy?
By whom was Judah defended against Shalmanezer?
Whose reign was longest?
Were the later Kings good men?
What became of Judah?
Who carried Judah away?

How long was Judah in captivity at Babylon?
How and under whom did they return?
On their return what did they do?
In what way did they live?
How long did they remain?

Notes. LATER, those who came after, subsequent. CHRONOLOGICAL, in the order of time. REVOLT, a nation refusing to obey its rulers. ANARCHY, disorder and no ruler. CONFUSION, misrule. ASSYRIA, a powerful land and nation east of Israel, near the rivers Euphrates and Tigris. BABYLON, one of the eldest cities of the world, the greatest then known. It was built on the river Euphrates and said to be 15 miles square, surrounded by walls and filled with gardens, palaces etc. CRUEL, hard hearted and unkind. REBELLED, fought against their King. IDOLATER, one who serves idols. LEPERS, persons afflicted with an incurable contagious disease of the skin from which they died forsaken as outcasts. REPAIRED, made good again. BONDAGE, slavery. RETURNED, came back. REBUILT, built again what had fallen. SUBJECT, obedient.

Lesson 24.—The Second Sunday after Easter.

A LESSON IN REVIEW.

COMMIT ISAIAH 52: 2, 3. READ PSALM 78. HEBREWS 11: 21—34.

THE STORY.

After Jacob's family (Israel) had dwelt in Egypt 216 years, the LORD raised up in Pharaoh's house, Moses, who set these poor slaves free. Ten plagues were sent upon Egypt who would not let Israel be free. Moses established the "Passover" feast, and, with Aaron his brother for High Priest with God, led the people away through the Red Sea. Moses also received the Ten Commandments on two tablets from the LORD, and set up the Tabernacle in the wilderness.

Israel wandered with Moses for forty years in the wilderness. On the border of the "Promised Land," Moses died; and Joshua led the people onward through the River Jordan. He also drove away the wicked Canaanites. He divided the land by lot among the twelve tribes. Joshua led Israel for twenty-five years.

When he died, the people were ruled by Elders and Judges, chief among whom were Othniel, Eglon, Barak, Gideon and Samson the strong. During these 271 years of the Judges, Ruth came with Naomi to Bethlehem, and married the pious and rich Boaz.

At the death of Eli the High Priest, Samuel, whom Eli had adopted and taught, became High Priest, Judge and Defender of Israel. Eli and Samuel ruled for sixty years.

Samuel anointed the brave, tall and handsome Saul as the first King of Israel. Saul drove away the Philistines and reigned for forty years. Then David, Ruth's great grandson, who, as a boy, had slain the giant Goliath, was King.

From his family the SAVIOUR was promised to come.

Solomon, the son of David, was a very wise, honored and rich King. With the wood, stone and metals gathered by his father, he built the beautiful Temple at Jerusalem.

David and Solomon each reigned for forty years.

Next came King Rehoboam, when ten Tribes turned away from the King of Judah and Benjamin, to make the new "Kingdom of Israel." Every King of Israel was an idolater. The Kingdom of Israel continued for only 254 years, when the people were carried as slaves to Assyria and never returned. The Kingdom of Judah had some pious Kings and remained for 387 years; when Jerusalem was taken and the people were carried away to Babylon, for a captivity of 70 years in all. (B. C. 606 to 536.) They then returned and held Jerusalem for 606 years, during which time the SAVIOUR came and died for our sakes. At last Jerusalem was destroyed by the Roman Titus A. D. 70. The time from Jacob's coming to Egypt to the destruction of Jerusalem is 1795 years.

REVIEW.

How long did Jacob's family dwell in Egypt?
How many tribes were there?
Whom did the LORD raise up to set the people free?
Can you describe how he succeeded?
What great acts did Moses perform?
Who next led the people?
Do you remember what good he did?
Can you name any of the Judges?
Who was the strong man?
Who lived at Bethlehem of Judea in those days?
Who was the High Priest after Eli?
Which two persons did he anoint to be Kings?
What wonderful promise was given to David?
Tell me something about Solomon and his acts.
What sad parting happened in Rehoboam's day?
What kind of Kings did Israel have?

How long did the kingdom of Israel last?
How was it destroyed?
Can you state anything concerning the kingdom of Judah?
How long did it remain?
What great trouble came upon it?
What did the people afterward do?
How long did they remain in Jerusalem?
What happened in Jerusalem toward the end of this time?
Who at last took Jerusalem?
How long is the period of our lesson?

Notes. RECEIVED, took, accepted. LOT, choice by chance. ELDERS, older men, leaders and heads of families.

Lesson 25.—The Third Sunday after Easter.

MORDECAI AND ESTHER.

COMMIT PROV. 16: 18, 19. READ THE BOOK OF ESTHER.

THE STORY.

Some of the Jews never returned from Babylon. Among these was noble Mordecai, a Benjamite. He reared his orphan cousin Esther, a pious and beautiful maid.

Vashti, the Queen of Ahasuerus of Babylon, was disobedient, so that the angry King sent her away. Then he chose Esther to be his Queen, because she was so fair and good.

Mordecai, who sat at the Kings gate, heard two men plot to kill the King and saved his life by telling him of it.

The King exalted Haman, an officer, to be his chief friend. Mordecai would not honor him, for he knew that Haman had a wicked heart. Haman hated Mordecai for this and bribed the King to kill every Jew on a certain day appointed by lot. The Jews heard the King's command with great weeping and distress.

Esther, looking out from her window, saw the Jews go about sorrowing, and sent to Mordecai to know what it meant.

After he had told her of the wicked Haman's plan, she made a feast for the King and invited only Haman, the Jews' enemy. Haman was glad to be the only honored guest. In his hate of Mordecai, Haman made a gallows, on which he might hang him whom he so despised.

That night the King could not sleep, so they read to him, from the records of his kingdom, the story of Mordecai saving the King's life. As a reward, the next day the King commanded, that Haman should lead the King's own horse for Mordecai to ride; to show to all how the grateful King delighted to honor the man who had saved his life. At a second feast of Haman with the King, Esther told Ahasuerus that by the plot of Haman, she and all her Jewish nation must die. The King was very angry. Haman pleaded in vain for life. The King commanded that he be hanged in the place he had prepared for Mordecai; while Mordecai wore the King's ring of state and a costly robe.

The Jews were saved by defending themselves. Ever since this event, on the same day of the year, a great feast has been kept, and called Purim, (lots,) because the LORD so wonderfully delivered the innocent people from destruction, and turned their sorrow into joy.

REVIEW.

Did all the captive Jews return to Jerusalem?
Of what tribe was Mordecai?
What was the name of his orphan cousin? Describe her.
What loving duty did faithful Mordecai perform?
What was Vashti's sin? What became of her?
Are princes always to be trusted? Ps. 118: 9.
What is a plot? How did Mordecai save the King's life?
Whom did Ahasuerus make his Queen?
Whom did the King raise to be his chief officer?
Why would not Mordecai honor Haman?
How did Haman feel toward Mordecai?
Was Haman revengeful? How?
Is revenge a sin? Romans 12: 19—21.
What great sentence passed upon all the Jews?
How did the Jews hear this command?
What did Queen Esther see?
What did she do?
To whom did she send an invitation to the feast?
What did Haman make?
A story was read to the sleepless King; what was it?
How did the grateful King at last honor Mordecai?
What happened at the second feast of Haman with the King and Queen?
How did the King feel when he found what Haman had been doing?
What was the end of cruel Haman?
How was Mordecai honored?

THE CAPTIVITY AND LATER HISTORY. 71

How were the Jews saved?
In honor of this event, what great annual feast do the Jews keep? Why?
What sins are shown by this lesson?
Are there any noble actions related? Ps. 103: 4.

Notes. REARED, brought up, trained. ORPHAN, deprived of parents. PLOT, to plan mischief. EXALTED, honored with a high office. BRIBED, unlawfully, paid for a favor. FEAST, a fine dinner. GUEST, one invited to a festival. GALLOWS, a machine for slaying a man by hanging. DESPISED, thought little of. RECORDS, true tales of the past. GRATEFUL, thankful. PLEADED, begged, asked very earnestly. VAIN, for nothing, to no purpose. DEFENDING, driving back the attack. EVENT, occurrence. OCCURRED, happened, took place. DELIVERED, set free. INNOCENT, harmless, guiltless. DESTRUCTION, ruin, death. JOY, happiness.

Lesson 26.—The Fourth Sunday after Easter.

THE CAPTIVITY AND LATER HISTORY.

COMMIT PS. 137: 1. JER. 2: 13. READ II. KINGS, II. CHRONICLES, EZRA, NEHEMIAH.

THE STORY.

721 years before CHRIST (B. C.), the idolatrous kingdom of Israel was, with Hoshea the last King, carried away by Shalmanezer the King of Assyria. Their land was filled and settled by strangers, idolaters, who were called "Samaritans". At that time Hezekiah was King of Judah. When Nebuchadnezzar became King at Babylon, B. C. 606, Jehoiakim, King of Judah, (who had been made to serve the King of Babylon,) rebelled. But the powerful King of Babylon sent an army and destroyed Judea, captured Jerusalem and took away many prisoners. He killed Jehoiakim, but made his son Jehoiachin to reign for three months. Nebuchadnezzar then came to Jerusalem, took the gold and furniture from the Temple of Solomon and carried away ten thousand people. He then gave the kingdom to Zedekiah, who reigned in his weak way till he also dared to rebel. Then Nebuchadnezzar broke down the city walls and burned the holy, beautiful Temple of Solomon. He now carried all the people away to Babylon, and the seventy years of the "Babylonian Captivity," which began B. C. 606 continued till B. C. 536.

Noble Cyrus became the King at Babylon and commanded the Temple at Jerusalem to be rebuilt. He sent back to Jerusalem 42,000 Jews, with Zerubbabel B. C. 536, who rebuilt the

72   THE CAPTIVITY AND LATER HISTORY.

Temple. Ezra and a new multitude followed B. C. 468, and Nehemiah B. C. 455, who led another host, rebuilt the city wall.

Tatnai and Sanballat, the Samaritans, were jealous and opposed the Jewish builders, but could not hinder them.

Rebuilding the Temple.

Thus we see that the LORD permitted the Jews to be overcome, because they were sinful. They were ruled by Babylon, B. C. 588; Alexander the Great, B. C. 330; Egypt, B. C. 320;

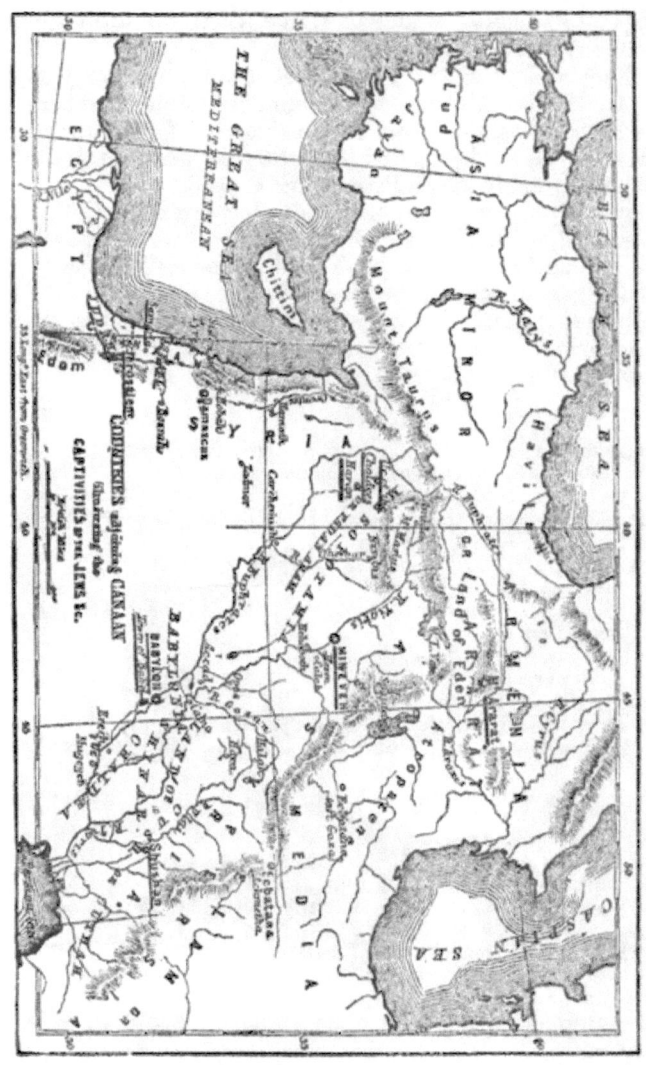

Syria, B. C. 170; and Pompey of Rome, B. C. 63, until the time of our Saviour's birth.

In the year 320 B. C. 100,000 captives were carried into Egypt. In 170 B. C. 40,000 were slain, the same number sold as slaves by Syrians, and the Temple was used for idolatry. But Judas Maccabeus, a hero, defeated the enemies, and Jonathan his brother was made High Priest. B. C. 163.

Pompey, the Roman general, took Jerusalem B. C. 63, and in the year B. C. 49, Herod I, or "the Great," was sent by Rome to be King over Judea. He took and plundered the city, but afterward began to build up Jerusalem.

In the year B. C. 31 Augustus Cæsar became Emperor of Rome, and was ruling over King Herod and Judea when the little Babe, JESUS, was born at Bethlehem.

REVIEW.

What was the sad end of Hoshea and wicked Israel?
Had they broken any great commandment?
How was their land settled?
What were these strangers named? Luke 10: 33. 17: 16.
Who was then King of Judah?
What powerful King reigned in Babylon B. C. 606?
Who rebelled against him?
What did Nebuchadnezzar do to the city, the Temple and the people of Jerusalem?
To what city did he take the Jews?
How long were they slaves?
What was their slavery called?
Who ordered the Temple to be rebuilt?
Can you mention three men who led the people home to Jerusalem.
Who rebuilt the Temple?
Who the city wall? Who opposed this?
Could they stop the building?
What nations conquered the Jews? Why?
How many were carried to Egypt at one time?
How many were slain and how many were sold into Syria at another time? Who defended Judah?
By what Roman general was Jerusalem taken?
To whom was the Kingdom of Judea given?
What did he do to the city?
Who was Emperor at Rome when JESUS was born?

Notes. SETTLED, used as a home. STRANGERS, people from far away. SAMARITANS, those who lived in the central part of the Holy Land, called Samaria, (the "mountain of watching") FURNITURE, articles needed for use in a house or Temple,

CAPTIVITY, slavery, bondage. ORDERED, gave command. JEWS, Judeans or those who dwelt in the Southern portion of the Holy Land, called Judea. HINDER, check, prevent, stop. SAVIOUR, one who helps or saves the sinner. PLUNDERED, seized, destroyed or carried off every precious thing.

Lesson 27.—The Fifth Sunday after Easter.

THE TEMPLES OF ISRAEL.

COMMIT HABAKKUK 2: 20. I. CORINTHIANS 3: 16, 17. READ I. KINGS 6—8. II. CHRON. 3—7. EZRA 3—6.

THE STORY.

The *Tabernacle*, (Less. 15, 16) remained at Shiloh until King David brought it to Jerusalem (Less. 21). After David had gathered the materials, King Solomon, in seven and a half years, (B. C. 1002—1004) built a magnificent and beautiful TEMPLE in Jerusalem, to serve instead of the Tabernacle. It was made of three courses of great hewn stones, with cedar beams above; all prepared before they were brought to the place, so that no sound of hammer, axe, or any tool was heard when the house was built.

In a large enclosure was first the *Porch*, 36 feet wide, 18 feet deep, having as supports two large pillars, named "Jachin" ("He shall establish") and "Boaz" ("in strength"). Within great doors, covered with gold, was *The Holy Place*, 72 by 36 feet, walled and ceiled with carved and gilded cedar. Here, supported on the backs of twelve bronze oxen, was a brazen *Basin*, or *Sea*, holding 15,000 gallons of water. Here were also *ten brazen Lavers* on their *ten Bases* of brass, also a *Table of Shewbread*, *ten Candlesticks* and an *Altar of Incense*, all of gold, beside golden *Bowls*, *Spoons*, *Censers*, one hundred *Basins* and other measures.

Within another door of cedar and a *Vail* was the *Oracle*, or *Most Holy Place*, 36 by 36 feet. Into this Oracle King Solomon and Israel brought the *Ark of the Covenant* and set it between two great gilded *Cherubim* of olive wood.

At the dedication by Solomon, "the cloud of the glory of the LORD filled the Temple," and the "Shekinah" appeared.

This splendid building stood perfect for 33 years only.

Then Shishak, King of Egypt came and plundered it.

Later it was pillaged by Kings Hazael of Syria, Tiglath Pileser and Sennacherib of Assyria.

It was destroyed B. C. 588 by Nebuchadnezzar. (Less. 26.)

After the Captivity, B. C. 536 (Less. 26) Zerubbabel and Jeshua built a less elegant Temple. But no Shekinah appeared in it. Antiochus Epiphanes, a Syrian conqueror, disgraced, (B. C. 163) but Judas Maccabeus (B. C. 160) restored and purified this second Temple.

It was afterward greatly repaired and improved by King Herod, and the Jews added precious gifts for forty-six years, before and during our Saviour's life. Into this Temple JESUS came.

This building, often called "Herod's Temple," was burned by Titus, the Roman general, when he took Jerusalem A. D. 70.

Besides the Temple at Jerusalem, the Jews in every place had houses of worship and instruction, called "Synagogues," and "places of prayer" on a hill top or the margin of a river.

The Christian Church, made up of believing and faithful souls, is God's real *Temple* now, and each heart should be also a Temple in itself.

REVIEW.

Where did the Tabernacle remain?
Who brought it to Jerusalem?
Who gathered the materials for a Temple?
Can you mention some of these materials?
Who built the first Temple to the LORD?
How long was it in building?
What was strange about its erection? I. Kings 6: 7.
Describe the Porch.   Describe the Holy Place.
What furniture was in the Holy Place? Matt. 27: 51.
Describe the Most Holy Place.
What was placed within it?
What happened at the dedication?
How long did the building stand perfect?
Who first plundered it?
By whom was it again plundered?
Who destroyed it?   Who built a second Temple? When?
Who disgraced this?   Who restored it?
Who repaired it?   John 2: 20. When was this?
Who made this Temple more holy than Solomon's by His presence? Haggai 2: 9. Mark 11: 15—17.
What became of Herod's Temple?

When did this occur?
What is now God's Temple? Eph. 2: 19—22.
What should each heart be? 1. Cor. 6: 19.

Notes. MATERIALS, substances used in building a house. MAGNIFICENT, of great appearance, grand. BEAUTIFUL, worthy of being admired. TEMPLE, a house and place kept from all worldly use for the worship of God; a Church. SERVE, to be useful. COURSES, layers. ENCLOSURE, a place shut in. PORCH, an open-sided building, with a roof supported by pillars. CEILED, finished as the top of a room. BRONZE, made of copper or brass; brazen. LAVERS, places for washing. SHEWBREAD, bread set as a grateful sign of God providing for His people. CENSERS, vessels used for burning incense. ORACLE, a secret place for God. CHERUBIM, figures of angels. PERFECT, complete. PILLAGED, ransacked. RESTORED, refilled, renewed, put again into place. BELIEVING, trusting, depending, knowing the truth.

Lesson 28.—The Sunday after Ascension.

THE PROPHETS AND THE TYPES OF CHRIST.

COMMIT THE TITLES OF THE BOOKS OF THE OLD TESTAMENT. READ Is. 53. DANIEL 9. ZECH. 9: 9—11. MAL. 3: 1. ACTS 10: 42, 43.

THE STORY.

In the days of the Judges and the Kings certain pious persons were teachers of holy things. To many of these good men the LORD gave wonderful wisdom, [called "Inspiration"] to see and say beforehand what would happen. They were called "Seers," or "Prophets." Their scholars were "Sons of the Prophets." The Prophets were sent by the LORD, to announce His blessing or warning to Judah, Israel and even to the nations round about and to prove it by working great miracles. Sometimes false prophets arose, who pretended to be inspired by the LORD. They were punished with death. Jesus often referred to the Prophets, and their grandest prophecies were concerning Him. Jesus is *"the* PROPHET," or Teacher of all men, the very "Word made Flesh."

Among the ancient Prophets may be mentioned *Moses* [died B. C. 1451], *Balaam* [1480, to whom the beast that carried him spake], *Deborah*, a prophetess [1291, who helped Barak], *Samuel* [1095, who was also High Priest], *David* [1015, who was also King], *Elijah* [896, who foretold drought, raised the widow's son, prayed and fire came from heaven to burn his sacrifice, divided the Jordan with his mantle, took leave of Elisha, and, like

Enoch went up to Jehovah (or the LORD), without dying; being carried away in a chariot of fire to heaven]. *Elisha*, [892, who received the mantle of Elijah and became his successor. He parted the Jordan with his mantle, purified the bitter water at

Elijah and the Prophets of Baal.

Jericho, was mocked by children who were killed by bears, prayed and obtained rain, multiplied the widow's oil, raised to life the son of the woman of Shunem, healed Naaman of his leprosy, anointed those who were to be Kings and performed many other wonderful works.]

THE PROPHETS AND THE TYPES OF CHRIST.

Many of the later Prophets also wrote Books of the Bible, probably in the following order: *Jonah*, [785, who was swallowed and cast up unhurt by a great fish.] *Amos*, [760 B. C.] *Hosea*, [725.] *Isaiah*, [712, whose greatest prophecies relate plainly to Christ.] *Micah*, [710.] *Nahum*, [700.] *Joel*, [690.] *Zeph-*

Elijah's Ascension.

aniah, [630.] *Habakkuk*, [590.] *Jeremiah*, [588, called the "weeping Prophet."] *Obadiah*, [587.] *Ezekiel*, [574.] *Daniel*, [536, a statesman of Babylon, who was cast into a den of lions, without harm.] *Haggai* and *Zechariah*, [520.] *Ezra*, [456.] *Nehemiah*, [433.] *Malachi*, [397.] with whom prophecy ceased.

80 THE PROPHETS AND THE TYPES OF CHRIST.

Of these, Isaiah, Jeremiah, Ezekiel and Daniel are called the greater and Hosea, Joel, Amos, Obadiah, Jonah, Micah, Nahum,

Jonah cast-up by a Whale.

Habakkuk, Zephaniah, Haggai, Zechariah and Malachi the minor (or less) prophets.

The Prophets and the Types of Christ. 81

Types are the holy persons, places or things, that, having been commanded by the LORD and connected with His covenant, point to CHRIST and remind us of Him.

And CHRIST is sometimes called the *Antitype*, because He is the One to Whom all Old Testament Types refer and point.

Of such Types are the Ark of Noah, the Law, the High Priest and his Atonement, the Passover, the Paschal Lamb,

Daniel in the Lion's Den.

the Judge, the Prophet, the King, the Tabernacle, the Temple, and its Sacrifices of Sin Offering and Peace Offering (for omissions of duty), First-fruits, the water of purifying; Light, Incense, Bread, the Mercy-seat, Shekinah. Also the brazen Serpent, Shepherd, Patriarch, Leader, Advocate, Conqueror, Manna, Rock; and such persons as Adam, Abraham, Melchizedek, Isaac, Moses, Joshua, David, Solomon, Jonah, etc.

REVIEW.

Who were the Prophets?
What great gifts were granted to some of them? I. Peter 1: 10—12.
What names were therefore given to them and their scholars? I. Sam. 10: 10; 19: 20.
What did the LORD often send them to do?
How could they prove that God had sent them?
How were false prophets punished? Deut. 18: 20. Jer. 27: 15—17. II. Peter 2: 1.
Who often referred to the Prophets? Compare Is. 42: 1—4 and Matt. 12: 18—21.
About Whom were the grandest prophecies spoken? Ps. 16: 8—11. 22: 18. 118: 22. Is. 61: 1, 2. Zech. 9: 9.
What title is therefore given to Jesus? John 1: 14. Acts 7: 37.
Can you mention the names of the Prophets?
Can you tell me anything about Balaam? Numbers 23: 26 &c. Moses? Deborah? Samuel? Acts 3: 24. David? Ps. 110: 1 and Matt. 22: 44. Elijah? I. Kings 17: 1. Elisha? II. Kings 2: 9—13. Jonah? Isaiah? Jeremiah? Daniel?
With whom did prophecy cease?
Which are the greater prophets?
Which are the minor prophets?
Did some of the prophets work miracles? Why?
Who gave them this power?
What are Types? To Whom do they refer?
In what part of the Bible do you find Types?
What is Jesus called, as represented by Types?
Can you mention some Types of Christ?
Do you see any reasons for comparing any of these Types with Christ?

Notes. TEACHERS, those who give instruction. WONDERFUL, astonishing. INSPIRATION, the "breathing" into man of Divine wisdom and power. HAPPEN, take place, occur. SEER, one who sees the future. ANNOUNCE, speak, or tell of. FALSE, not true, or real. REFERRED, carried back in thought. DROUGHT, dryness, want of rain. MANTLE, a cloak. CHARIOT, an ancient carriage or car. SUCCESSOR, one who takes the place of another. PARTED, divided. MOCKED, abused by ridicule, pretended to honor.

PART SECOND.

THE NEW TESTAMENT.

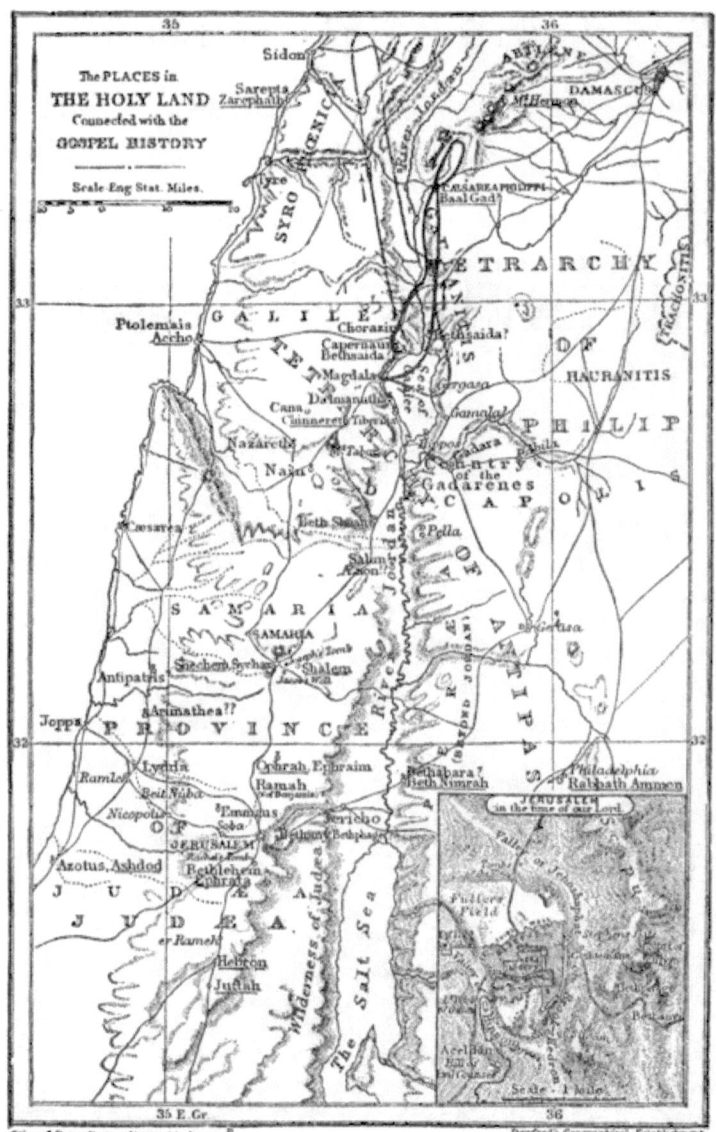

Lesson 29.—Whit Sunday.

PREPARATION.

JOHN THE BAPTIST AND HIS MESSAGE.

COMMIT JOHN 1: 6, 7, 8. READ LUKE 1 and 7: 19—35. Matt. 14: 1—12.

THE STORY.

While Cæsar Augustus was Emperor of Rome, he appointed Herod to be King of Judea in his name. In the days of King Herod it fell, by lot, to a certain good and faithful old priest, Zacharias to burn incense at the Altar in the Temple and offer prayer at the set hour of prayer. While so doing, a glorious angel, Gabriel, appeared by his side and told him that his pious childless wife Elizabeth should bear a son; to be named John. This son, said the angel, "shall go before the LORD," like Elijah, to prepare the people to receive their Saviour.

As a sign of this the mistrusting Zacharias was to be speechless till the child was named. The son, when born, was named "John," as the angel had said. The people asked, "What manner of child shall this be? for the LORD is with him." When John was circumcised, Zacharias recovered his speech, and prophesied, saying, "Thou, child, shalt be called the prophet of the Highest."

John grew to be strong in the Spirit of the LORD. He lived alone in the wilderness till he was about thirty years of age. Then, clad in a coarse robe of camel's hair, and girt with a leathern belt, the solitary man came forth to teach.

His food was locusts and the honey made by the wild bees. Those who came to listen, he taught to be sorry for their sins; and repenting, to be baptized by him at the Jordan, to show that they were both truly sorry for their evil hearts and bad lives; and also needed a Saviour who could take away their sins. He taught and baptized the crowds that soon came out to hear him, so as to prepare the people for their coming Saviour.

And when John at length saw Jesus, he said, "Behold the Lamb of God which taketh away the sin of the world."

Afterward John spoke against the great sins of King Herod, grandson of Herod the great, who had married his brother Philip's wife. For this the holy John was shut up in prison. Finally to please the daughter of Philip's wife, Herod sent and cut off the head of John the Baptist in the prison. John's disciples sadly took his body and buried it.

The difference between John's baptism and Christian baptism is that John's baptism showed that all *needed* cleansing from sin and promised it unto them. Christian baptism *is* the cleansing of the LORD and the remission of sin.

REVIEW.

What great Emperor and noted Kings are mentioned in our Lesson?
Do we speak of any priest? Luke 1: 5, 6.
Can you describe him and Elizabeth his wife?
What was his duty at this time?
Should Christians have an hour of prayer?
Who appeared to Zacharias and what was his glad message? Luke 1: 13—19.
What name was to be given to the child?
What sign was given to prove the message true?
Tell about the naming of John.
What was the covenant act performed upon John? Lesson 6.
Did his father foretell anything about John?
How did John spend the greater part of his life? Luke 1: 80.
When thirty years old what did he do?
Was he dressed with great splendor?
Upon what did he live?
Did many come to him?
Why did they come?
What did he tell them?
What is it to repent?
Should all repent? Should they do this daily?
What did repenting show?
What did John also do to the people? Matt. 3: 1—3.
Should not those who repent also try to live better? Is. 55: 7. Rom. 12: 9.
Why did John baptize the people?
What is *Baptism*? See Catechism Part IV.

Were you baptized?
What did John say of Jesus?
Was Jesus baptized by John?   Luke 3: 21, 22.
Of Whom did John bear witness?   John 3: 28.
Did John ever claim that he himself was Christ? No! John 1: 20–27.
What did he declare about Jesus?   John 1: 29.   3: 31, 35, 36.
Why was John imprisoned?
How did he die?   For whose sake was it so?
What was done with his body?   Mark 6: 21—29.
What is the difference between John's baptism and Christian baptism?
Should *all* be baptized?

Notes. EMPEROR, the ruler over many lands. HOUR OF PRAYER, the time of daily worship. GLORIOUS, bright and honorable. APPEARED, came into sight. JOHN, a name signifying "the Grace of the LORD." PREPARE, make ready. MISTRUSTING, having but little faith. SPEECHLESS, silent, dumb. MANNER, style. RECOVERED, gained again. SPIRIT, the Third Person of the Holy Trinity, the power of all the good in the world. LOCUSTS, insects, used as food when dried, or parched by the poor. DISCIPLES, devoted followers, scholars, learners.

The Annunciation.

Lesson 30.—Trinity Sunday.

INCARNATION.

THE COMING AND CHILDHOOD OF JESUS THE CHRIST.

Commit Isaiah 9: 6. John 1: 14. Read Luke 1: 26—56. Matt. 1: 18 to 2: 23.

THE STORY.

Joseph, a carpenter, and Mary, his promised bride, dwelt in Nazareth of Galilee. The angel Gabriel was sent to pious Mary to say, that, like her cousin Elizabeth, a son would be

The Angel-message.

given to her. But Mary's child would be the "Son of God" so long promised. Joseph also, in a dream, received word that Mary's holy CHILD would be placed in his care as His foster-father; and that he should name Him JESUS; for He would save His people from their sins.

With other nations Augustus Cæsar taxed all the Jews. Joseph and Mary, his future wife, went from Nazareth to Bethlehem of Judea, for both belonged to the family of King David and must be taxed there. While in Bethlehem, being very poor and the inn crowded, they lodged in a stable. Here, as had been promised, *the* CHRIST-CHILD *was born.* He was swathed and had a manger for His cradle.

On that same night in a meadow near the town some shepherds were quietly watching their flocks, when lo! a glorious angel came to tell them that CHRIST the SAVIOUR of the world

The Adoration of the Shepherds.

was born! Then a multitude of angels were seen, singing "Glory to God in the highest and on earth peace good will toward men."

The shepherds soon ran to Bethlehem and found Joseph and Mary with the holy CHILD. They praised God and told many about their message.

On the eigth day after His birth the CHILD was circumcised and received His name JESUS, or *"Saviour"*. When He was forty days old His parents went up with Him to Jerusalem, six miles away, to present Him to the LORD in His holy Temple. Here two pious old people, Simeon and Anna, foretold that this was the "Wonderful Child, Who would save all men."

After the CHILD had been carried back to Bethlehem, wise men, called "Magi", led by a star, came from the East to Jerusalem, asking King Herod and the Jews where they might find the new CHILD-KING. The star again led them till in Bethle-

The Presentation.

hem they found Him. They offered to Him gifts of gold, frankincense and myrrh.

King Herod, hearing of all this, feared that this CHILD would grow and take away his kingdom. Joseph, warned by the LORD in a dream about Herod, took away from Bethlehem to Egypt the CHILD and His mother. Thus Joseph saved His life, for Herod sent and slew all the little children of Bethlehem, thinking that he would surely kill the new-born CHILD, JESUS.

At last Joseph and Mary came home to Nazareth with their little Son; and *Jesus* grew up to help Joseph at his work, and was obedient and good.

When JESUS was twelve years old, His parents took Him with them to Jerusalem, to the Temple, to have Him united with the Church. His parents, supposing Him with them among a

Joseph warned by the Lord in a Dream.

large company of friends and fellow travelers, started homeward, and JESUS was left behind alone in Jerusalem. After three sorrowful days of seeking they found Him in the Temple, hearing and understanding the wise old teachers; asking and answering questions with so great skill that all wondered at Him.

REVIEW.

Mention who lived in Nazareth. Who was sent to Mary? Tell his message. How would Mary's child be called? Had He been promised? Gen. 3: 15. Is. 7: 14. How did God speak to Joseph?

By what name should Mary's CHILD be known?
What would JESUS do? Matt. 1: 21.
Augustus Cæsar gave a great command, what was it?
Did Joseph and Mary obey?
To what place did they come?
How did they lodge? Why?
As they tarried there what took place?
Had this been promised? Micah 5: 2.
How did they care for the little CHILD?
Tell what some pious shepherds in the fields heard and saw.
Did the angels sing a beautiful hymn?
Can you repeat it? Luke 2: 14.
Did the shepherds go to see the CHILD?
Were they glad to find Him?
What happened on the eighth day of JESUS' life? Matthew 1: 21. Luke 2: 21.
To what great house was He taken when forty days old?
Did any one there prophesy concerning Him? Luke 2: 25—38.
Who came to Jerusalem? Matt. 2: 1—12.
Was Jesus in the city then?
How were they led? What did they ask?
To what place did the star again lead them?
Did they find Jesus? What gifts did they offer?
Why did Herod fear when he heard of this CHILD?
To what land did Joseph take Mary and Jesus?
What sad, rash act soon happened in Bethlehem?
To what town did Joseph at last return? How did JESUS grow?
What happened when He was twelve years old?
For what was He taken to Jerusalem?
What mistake occurred? How long did they lose JESUS?
How were those days spent? Was He found? In what place?
Why did all the teachers wonder at JESUS?
Do you know why He was so wise? Luke 2: 41—52. I. Corinth. 1: 24, 30.

Notes. INCARNATION, the act of becoming a human being; taking a body. TRINITY, Tri-unity; or the title of the union of the Three Persons, Father, Son and Holy Ghost in one Godhead. NAZARETH OF GALILEE, in Herod's day the Holy Land was divided into three parts, Galilee (North), Samaria (Centre), Judea (South), Nazareth was a despised town in the district of Galilee. SON OF GOD, the second person of the Godhead, Who was promised to come to earth in human form to save man. DREAM, a thought or idea during sleep. FOSTER-FATHER, one who acts as a father for an adopted child. JESUS, a name meaning "God is Saviour." AUGUSTUS, the first or greatest Cæsar, or Roman Emperor. He reigned for 44 years. TAXED, commanded to pay to the government. BETHLEHEM OF JUDEA, a hamlet in the southern part of the Holy Land, six miles south of Jerusalem. BELONGED, pertained to. LODGED, dwelt for a short time. STABLE, a hut, (or perhaps better a cave) for sheltering cattle. INN, a public house for travelers to tarry. CHRIST, a name signifying "The Anointed One." SWATHED, wound in bands to ensure straight limbs. MANGER, a trough for feeding cattle. GIFTS, presents. GOLD, the most precious metal then known; a sign of JESUS' kingly nature. FRANKINCENSE, a sweet resin burned in a censer; a sign of JESUS' priestly office. MYRRH, a fragrant gum used in burial; a prophecy of JESUS' death. SKILL, knowing how to say or do a thing.

The Baptism and Temptation of Jesus.   93

Lesson 31.—The First Sunday after Trinity.

CONSECRATION.
THE BAPTISM AND TEMPTATION OF JESUS.

Commit I. Peter 3: 13—15. Read Matt. 3 and 4: 1—11. Mark 1: 1—13. Luke 3: 21—23. 4: 1—15.

THE STORY.

While John was teaching and baptizing, Jesus came down from Nazareth of Galilee, also to be baptized of John. Jesus

John baptizing Jesus.

was now about thirty years old. John would not at first baptize Jesus with his Baptism unto repentance and preparation. But the Lord Jesus showed that John's Baptism of Him pointed Him out as the *Saviour*, and consecrated Him for the work He would do. Thus He became an example to all who follow Him and thus He fulfilled His duty.

Then John baptized Jesus; and lo! as Jesus prayed, the heavens opened and the Spirit of God came in the form of a dove, and rested on Him; while the voice of God the Father said from above, "This is my beloved Son in Whom I am well pleased."

The Spirit of the LORD now led Jesus into the wilderness of Judea. Here He remained for forty days having nothing to eat. Then Satan the tempter came to Him, urging Him to do what Satan wished, by changing the stones into bread; for Christ could do any-thing that He wanted to do, being the Son of God. But Jesus said to Satan: "It is written, Man shall not live by bread alone, but by every word that proceedeth out of the mouth of God."

But Satan again tried to tempt the LORD. He led Jesus to Jerusalem, till they stood upon a pinnacle at the top of the Temple. "If you are the Son of God," said wicked Satan, "as you claim to be, cast down yourself, for the word of God says He shall give His angels charge concerning thee, and in their hands they shall bear thee up; lest, at any time thou dash thy foot against a stone." Jesus also said, "It is written, Thou shalt not tempt the LORD thy God."

And Satan, the great enemy, tried even the third time to tempt Jesus by taking Him to the top of a high mountain, to show Him what a great world this is, with its kingdoms and glory; yet all lying in sin. "All these will I give Thee, if Thou wilt fall down," said the arrogant impostor, "and worship me." But Jesus overcame this last temptation by remembering the Word of God where it is written: "Thou shalt worship the LORD thy God, and Him only shalt thou serve."

Then the devil departed; and holy, heavenly angels came to minister unto Jesus, Who had now finished the trial of His power.

Afterward Jesus returned to Galilee.

REVIEW.

What was John the Baptist doing?
Who came to John to be baptized by him?
From what place did He come?

The Baptism and Temptation of Jesus.

How old was He at that time?
Should all be baptized? Matt. 23: 19. Mark 16: 16.
Was John willing at first to baptize Jesus?
Why do you think he was unwilling?
How did Jesus explain John's duty to Him?
What would John's Baptism show Jesus to be?
What would it do to Jesus?
What does "consecrate" mean?
How is Jesus our example? Matt. 3: 15.
Did John then baptize Jesus?
A wonderful event now took place, what was it?
Tell what was seen. Tell what was heard.
How did the Holy Spirit chose Jesus from all others?
How many persons of the Godhead are here revealed?
To what place was Jesus now led?
How long did He there remain?
What was strange concerning His life in the wilderness?
Did any-one come to Him there?
How was Jesus first urged to yield by Satan?
Can Jesus do all things?
How did Jesus answer Satan? Deut. 8: 3.
Who is the Bread of life for us? John 6: 48—50.
Could not Jesus have lived forever without eating?
Can we live forever without Jesus and His Truth? John 15: 5.
How did Satan again try Jesus? What is it to tempt?
On what did they now stand?
What did the devil, (Satan) ask Jesus to do?
How did he prove his request? Ps. 91: 11, 12.
Does God love those who abuse the Bible to help a bad cause?
Could Jesus conquer Satan again? Why?
How did He do it? Deut. 6: 16.
By the use of what Book may all temptation to sin be overcome?
Did Satan offer Jesus a third temptation? How?
How did the Son of God grandly overcome and defeat the adversary?
Deut. 6: 13. 10: 20. 1st Com.
As the Lord Himself has taught us, what should we pray concerning temptation?
At Satan's departure, who came to attend the Lord?
To what country did Jesus later return?

Notes. Consecration, setting one apart, by God's command, for a holy work or use. Baptism, the Sacrament of Regeneration and Adoption, which admits the believer to the Covenant of Grace with God. Temptation, trying the strength of one's faith or virtue. Preparation, making ready. Example, a pattern. Fulfilled, did what was promised. Spirit of God, the Holy Spirit, the Third Person of the Trinity. Form, the shape, or appearance. Beloved, well thought of. Pleased, satisfied, or contented. Remained, stayed, dwelt. Tempter, one who tries to destroy our virtue. Pinnacle, a high place on the roof of a building. Claim, to declare one's possession of a thing. Kingdoms, lands and people ruled by Kings. Arrogant, proud selfsufficient, contemptuous. Impostor, a deceiver with a false claim. Devil, (slanderer) man's great enemy Minister, serve, wait upon, do good for another.

Lesson 32.—The Second Sunday after Trinity.

INSTRUCTION AND INSTITUTION.

OUR LORD TEACHING AND SENDING FORTH HIS DISCIPLES.

Commit Acts 1: 1 and 2. Read Matt. 10: 1—11. 13: 1—23. Mark 6: 7—13. Luke 6: 12—19.

THE STORY.

Jesus Christ our Lord, soon after His Baptism and Temptation began to teach the people about God His Father and Himself, the Son of the Father. He came from Heaven to save all those who are sorry for their sins, turn from their wicked ways and in faith join His Kingdom called the Church.

He often taught them of heavenly things by a story of natural things. Such a story is called a "Parable." Many of Jesus' parables are recorded in the Bible. For instance, He told of a sower scattering seed; some on the trodden path, where it was crushed by passing feet or eaten by birds; some on stony ground, where it was soon dried up; some on ground full of thornroots, where it was choked; and some on good ground, where the seed soon took root, sprang up and brought forth fruit; thirty, sixty and even a hundred times what was sown.

People's hearts are the ground and the seed is the living truth taught by Jesus. Worldly hearts, like the beaten path, reject Jesus and His words and will not believe Him. Stony hearts pretend to learn and obey; but grow tired and soon cease from trying to serve Jesus the Sower. Others, like the thorny places, try to have both good and bad in their hearts, till the bad ways outgrow the good and the words of Jesus are forgotten. Others are like the good soil, for they believe what Jesus teaches, and try to understand His parables, open their willing hearts to receive the truth and try to keep on in doing right as the Lord has told them.

The holy Master and Teacher soon gathered many friends and learners, called "Disciples," who went with Him from place to place to hear His precious words of wisdom, to learn how to pray, and to be taught about everlasting life in the Kingdom of Heaven by union with Himself.

Once Jesus went up to a mountain spot, and continued all night in prayer with His Father. He then chose twelve of His disciples, whom He named "Apostles," and gave them command

Jesus Teaching His Disciples.

to go forth to teach of Him, and to gather in and baptize the people of the world for the Church of Christ. Jesus also gave special powers to the Apostles of speaking, of healing the sick, of casting out evil spirits that vexed the people in those days and of bringing back the dead to life. By this they could prove that God was with them. They went forth everywhere, though not at first to the Samaritans, because those people were not yet ready (willing), to receive the truth about Jesus.

The twelve Apostles were Simon, called Peter, and his brother Andrew; James and his brother John; Philip and Nathanael (or Bartholomew); Levi, called Matthew; Thomas; James (the son of Alphæus, sometimes called James the less); Thaddeus (or Lebbæus, or Judas); Simon (called the zealous), and Judas Iscariot (who was a traitor to Jesus).

These Apostle-disciples the Lord Jesus sent forth two and two. He helped them and they were very useful in establishing the Church.

REVIEW.

Was Jesus a teacher? Matt. 22 16. John 3: 2,
About what did He teach?
For what did He come from Heaven?
What is a parable? How did Jesus use parables?
In what Book do we find them?
Can you mention one? Matt. 13: 3—8.
How many kinds of ground are spoken of?
How are these like people's hearts?
Should not each have a good heart?
Which must be taken away to make the heart good?
What is like the precious seed?
What is more precious; a seed, or the truth?
Which is best in the end, virtue or sin?
Are there not sometimes found hypocrites and traitors even in the Church?
Is one mentioned in our lesson?
How should good hearts receive Jesus' words?
Whom did our Lord gather to Himself?
Why did the disciples follow Jesus?
What solemn act of worship did Jesus once perform?
After this what did He do?
How many did He chose?
Why did He chose them?
What did He call them?
How did He help these first missionaries?
In Whose name and by Whose authority alone could they teach and heal?
Why did they not at once go to the Samaritans?
Can you mention the names of the Apostles?
Did any of them ever heal the sick, cast out devils or raise the dead? Acts 3: 1—8. 5: 15, 16. 9: 34—41. 16: 16—18.
How were they sent out? Eph. 2: 20.

THE MIRACLES OF JESUS. 99

Notes. INSTRUCTION, the filling of the mind with facts. INSTITUTION, establishing, causing a thing to stand on a firm foundation. LORD, a Master. CHURCH, the Kingdom of Christ. HEAVENLY, like the Lord and His angels, sinless, pure, holy. PARABLE, a story of natural things to explain spiritual facts. CRUSHED, broken and destroyed by grinding. CHOKED, checked or stopped in growth and life. TIRED, weary. UNDERSTAND, to have a clear knowledge of a thing. GATHERED, collected. LEARNERS, those who seek instruction. EVERLASTING, able to endure forever. CONTINUED, stayed, remained, unchanged. APOSTLE, (sent out) a missionary, one whom Jesus sent to teach and baptize in His name. SPECIAL, particular. EVIL SPIRITS, demons, bad spirits that filled the minds of men with evil. PROVE, to show the truth of a fact or saying.

Lesson 33.—The Third Sunday after Trinity.

ACTION.

THE MIRACLES OF JESUS.

COMMIT ST. JOHN 20: 30, 31. READ ST. MATTHEW 8: 23 TO 9: 35.

THE STORY.

Jesus went about with His disciples from city to city in the Holy Land, in order to teach the people that He is indeed the Son of God having power to forgive sins and to lay down His life and take it again. He came to save the souls of all men, by the sacrifice of His own life for their sakes. He loved and blessed little children, and took them into His arms.

In order to prove that He was the Son of God and that His teaching was true and perfect, He performed miracles.

A miracle is a wonderful act done not by the laws of Nature, but above Nature by the direct power of God.

The miracles which Jesus did show us that He had power over, (1.) Nature; as for example, turning the water into wine at the marriage feast in Cana of Galilee; filling the nets with fish, feeding the multitudes with a few loaves and fishes, calming the storm etc; (2.) the Body of man; as when He made the blind to see, the lame to walk, the weak to be strong, the deaf to hear, the lepers to be cleansed; (3.) the Soul of man; for He drove out evil spirits and forgave the sins of men; (4.) the Life; by causing the dead to live again. All these He did to show that He was Christ the Son of God; Who could forgive sins and save our souls, if we will believe in Him.

For instance, as He was teaching at Capernaum, by the Sea of Galilee, Jairus, a certain ruler of the Synagogue, whose twelve year old daughter lay dying, came, humbly to ask Jesus to go home with him, and make his child well.

Jesus went. So did His disciples and a crowd with them.

On the way, a poor woman in the company, who had been ill for twelve years, came behind Jesus and touched His cloak.

So great was her faith in Jesus that she had said to herself: "If I can only touch the hem of His garment I shall be well." She *was* made well at once. But Jesus, Who knew all

The Marriage in Cana.

things, turned and asked, "Who touched Me?" The disciples, who saw the crowd, said, "All the people are pressing Thee." But the thankful woman came, trembling and bowing down, and told the Lord of her act. Jesus said to her, "Daughter, thy faith hath made thee whole, go in peace."

As He said this, a sad messenger came, to tell Jairus that his daughter was dead. It seemed in vain to ask Jesus for help now. But Jesus came into the house of the ruler, and, taking the parents with Peter, John and James, He said to the little girl as He took her hand in His: "Maiden, I say unto thee, arise." And the daughter did rise and live to the joy of all, and was well. So they gave her something to eat.

The Draught of Fishes.

Such were the beautiful works of power and love done by our dear Lord and Master, Jesus Christ; Who went about continually and Whose praise spread abroad into all that land.

REVIEW.

Why did Jesus go with His disciples from place to place?
What great special power did He have?
Of what benefit was it to men that He laid down His life? Matt. 28: 18. 9: 6, 7. John 10: 17, 18,
How did Jesus prove His power and Divine nature?
Can you tell what a miracle is?
By Whose presence and power alone can a miracle be performed?
Tell me, over what four parts of the present order of things did Jesus display His power.

The Miracles of Jesus.

Can you mention any miracles over Nature? The Body? The Soul? The Life?
Can Jesus, Who did these miracles, also save us?
Why were they done? 1. John 1: 1. 4: 2.
What is our great duty to Him? Matt. 11: 28—30.
For instance, where was Jesus teaching by the Sea?
What Sea? Who came to Jesus?
Had he a title? But how did he ask Jesus?
What trouble had Jairus?

Feeding the Multitude.

Did he ask a favor of Jesus? What?
Did Jesus go? Did others go?
In the crowd, who came behind Jesus?
What had she been? What did she do?
How did she reason to herself?
Was she made well? But what did Jesus do?
How did the disciples speak of the matter?
And what did the woman do?
Did Jesus tell her why she was made well?

What beautiful words did Jesus use?
In what spirit could the trembling woman depart?
What sad message came to Jairus?
What was hopeless now? But did Jesus go away?
What did He do? Whom did He take with Him?
What did He do and say to the little girl?
What was the result?
Ought we and all men to believe in Jesus?
What was He continually doing?
What shall we have, if we believe in Him? John 20: 31.
Did His fame spread abroad in that land?
Should not we do good for Jesus as well as believe in Jesus? James 2: 18.

Notes. ACTION, deeds, works. HOLY LAND, the land where our holy Saviour lived. SAKE, benefit, advantage. PERFORMED, did, worked. LAWS, rules, principles that govern. NATURE, the world with its powers. MULTITUDES, many people crowded together. CALMING, quieting. CLEANSED, made pure, or sound. CAPERNAUM, a town by the Sea of Galilee, which the Lord Jesus made "his own city," Matt. 9: 1, after the people of Nazareth had cast him out. Luke 4: 16, and 28, 29. RULERS OF THE SYNAGOGUE, wise and faithful Jews having charge of the synagogue. GARMENT, a cloak, robe, or mantle. MESSENGER, one who brings a message, or news. IN VAIN, to no purpose. PARENTS, the nearest of kin; father and mother.

Lesson 34.—The Fourth Sunday after Trinity.

MANIFESTATION.

THE TRANSFIGURATION OF JESUS.

COMMIT ST. JOHN 1: 5.　I. JOHN 1: 5.　READ ST. MATT. 17: 1—13.
ST. MARK 9: 2—13.　ST. LUKE 9: 28—36.

THE STORY.

One of the most wonderful of all Jesus' acts on earth is that which is called His Transfiguration. It showed that though He was truly a man, He was also truly the Son of God. Doubtless it took place on the eve of the Sabbath day. Jesus took Peter, James and John to the top of a high mountain, to pray. While there, His whole appearance became beautiful and splendid. His face shone as the Sun, and His garments were as bright as the light for whiteness. Also there were seen Moses, the Lawgiver, and Elijah the Prophet. Both these men had of old pointed to Christ Jesus, and now, in the glory of Jesus' presence, they spoke of His death for sinful man, soon to be fulfilled at Jerusalem.

The disciples were dull with sleep, but, rousing up at this great sight they saw the Lord before them with Moses and Elijah.

After the Law-giver and Prophet appeared, Peter said: "Master, it is good for us to be here. Let us make here three resting places, for Thee, for Moses and for Elijah." He could

The Transfiguration of Jesus.

not think of any better thing to say, than to ask to make booths that all might remain.

But while he spoke, a bright cloud came and covered them, and the voice of God the Father said from the cloud: "This is My beloved Son in Whom I am well pleased! Hear Him."

The disciples, full of fear, fell on their faces to the earth.

The Transfiguration of Jesus.

But Jesus came and touched them, saying: "Arise and be not afraid."

They looked up and saw only Jesus their Lord. The vision was ended. And the next day, as they came down from the mountain, Jesus gave them command not to speak of this great sign of His being the Son of God, till He was risen from the dead. For the people could not yet believe such great things as this event concerning Him. So the disciples kept this sight to themselves, wondering what Christ could mean by His rising from the dead.

REVIEW.

Mention one of the most wonderful of all Jesus' acts.
What do you think "transfigure" means?
Does His Transfiguration teach us anything about Jesus?
When did it doubtless occur?
Whom did Jesus take with Him to a mountain?
For what solemn duty did they go?
During their stay what happened?
Describe the change in the appearance of Jesus? St. John 1: 14.
Who also appeared?
What title is given to Moses? Less. 13 and 14. Why?
What title does Elijah have? Why? See Less. 28. I. Kings 17 to II. Kings 2.
Of Whom had these men before spoken?
Of what did they now specially speak?
Where was this to be fulfilled?
Was not this also a prophecy?
In what condition were the disciples at this time?
Rousing up, what great sight did they see?
Did Peter speak? What did he say?
Why did he say this?
While he spoke what came and covered them all?
Whose voice was heard? What was said?
Does this teach us anything concerning Jesus?
Had these words ever been heard from heaven before? Less. 31.
Should we give attention to the words of Jesus? II. Peter 1: 16—18.
What effect had the voice upon the disciples?
But Who came to them?
What did He do and say?
Looking up Whom did they see?
When did they come from the mountain?
What command did Jesus give them? Why?
Did the disciples obey?
But concerning what did they wonder?
Do you not believe that Jesus is the Son of God?

If you compare the vision of the Voice, the Christ, and the Cloud have you not a beautiful sign of the Holy Trinity, Father, Son and Holy Ghost?

Notes. MANIFESTATION, a showing, or making plain. It is the same as the Greek word Epiphany. TRANSFIGURATION, the change in the appearance of a person; the shining of the glory of God through the person of Jesus. APPEARANCE, the look, outward form, or view presented by a person. SPLENDID, brilliant, glorious. LAW-GIVER, one who received and read God's law for men. GLORY, honorable brightness. PRESENCE, the nearness of a person to you. JERUSALEM, the Capital City of the Jews; established by King David upon Mts. Zion, Moriah, Acra and Bezetha; containing the Temple, Palace, Towers, Homes and many buildings; all within great walls. ROUSING, awaking, starting up. BOOTHS, temporary houses, often made of boughs. SIGN, proof token. RISEN, having come up. EVENT, that which took place, a result. MEAN, intend, have in mind.

Lesson 35.—The Fifth Sunday after Trinity.

PASSION.

THE SUFFERINGS AND DEATH OF JESUS.

COMMIT ISAIAH 53: 4, 5. READ MATT. 21: 1—27. 24: 1—42. 26. 27. MARK 11 TO 15. LUKE 19: 28—48. 21. 22. 23. JOHN 12 TO 19. I. COR. 11: 23—25.

THE STORY.

JESUS, though the Son of God, came into this world to die for sinners, so that by giving Himself to all who will believe His word and take Him as their Saviour, He might grant eternal life.

On the Sunday before the Festival of the Passover, Jesus rode triumphantly as a King, yet meekly, into Jerusalem, while a great multitude strewed the way with garments spread out, or waved branches of palm. Going into the Temple, Jesus found there those who bought and sold oxen, sheep, doves and exchanged money for greedy gain. He drove all these away from His Father's "House of Prayer."

The jealous Jews hated Jesus because of His power. During the last week at Jerusalem, our Master taught His disciples many things both by parable and advice; and told them that Jerusalem would be destroyed.

The Chief Priests now laid plans to kill the loving Jesus,

Jesus Enters Jerusalem.

Judas Iscariot was bribed to betray Him in a dark and lonely hour.

When Thursday evening was come, the Passover supper was made ready. Jesus set an example of humility, by washing the feet of the disciples. He pointed out Judas as the traitor, who, soon after, went away. At the eating of the Passover, Jesus took bread and, giving thanks to God, broke it, and gave it to each, saying: "Take, eat, this is My body, which is given for you." "This do in remembrance of Me." Also, at the close of the Supper, He took the cup of thanksgiving and, blessing God, handed it to them, and said: "Drink all ye of it;" (and all drank of it,) "for this cup is the New Testament in My Blood, which is shed for you," and the many souls of all the world, "for the remission of sins." Thus instead of the ancient Jewish Passover, our Lord established a new Supper of Life for Christians to keep.

The Lord's Supper Instituted.

After the Supper they talked, prayed and sang a hymn together. The disciples then followed their Master out of the city, to "Gethsemane", a garden on the Mount of Olives. Here, while waiting for His enemies, Jesus was engaged in prayer; so earnest, that "His sweat was, as it were, great drops of blood falling down to the ground."

It was about midnight when Judas led the soldiers of the jealous High Priest to this spot; and kissed Jesus, to show the

The Sufferings and Death of Jesus. 109

men which was his Master. They took Jesus, bound Him and carried Him away to Annas, an old High Priest. Then, early in the morning of the day now called "Good Friday," they led Jesus to Caiaphas, the High Priest that year. The disciples fled away. The Sanhedrim, or Jewish High Council met very early, and judged the holy Jesus guilty and worthy of death. Then the people mocked Him.

They now led Christ Jesus to Pontius Pilate, the Roman

Jesus before Annas.

Governor, to ask him to agree with their jugdment and to order that Jesus be put to death, while Judas repenting, came and threw back to the Chief Priests their bribe-money, and went and put himself to death by hanging.

Pilate wished to set Jesus free, he sent Him to Herod, King of Galilee, who was then in Jerusalem. But Herod sent Him back to Pilate for another trial, and neither could find any fault in Him, save that He said He was the "King of the Jews," though His Kingdom was not of this world. At last, to please the Jews, Pilate gave orders to scourge Jesus and finally delivered Him to be crucified with two thieves. After being mocked, by having to wear a crown of plaited thorns and a soldier's faded scarlet robe, He was led out of the city gates to a place called "Calvary," and crucified between the two thieves, on a cross, to which His hands and feet were nailed. Over His head they

Jesus before Pilate.

put this writing: "JESUS OF NAZARETH, THE KING OF THE JEWS." Even on the cross He was mocked by those who passed by. His mother, Mary, who stood with others at the cross weeping, He gave into the care of His disciple John. He prayed for His enemies: "Father forgive them, for they know not what they do."

While Jesus was dying, darkness spread over the earth, from noon until three in the afternoon. Then it was that

Jesus bowed His holy Head and died; for man, the creature's sin.

The Crucifixion on Mount Golgotha or Calvary.

At once, the Vail of the Temple was rent from top to bottom! There was a great earthquake, and many, who had been dead arose, and were seen in Jerusalem! The Roman captain, when he saw all this, said: "Truly this was the Son of God!"

The soldiers, finding Jesus dead, pierced His side; and from it came both blood and water. The body of Jesus was taken down by Joseph and Nicodemus, wrapped in linen and laid in a sepulchre, or tomb cut in a rock; till the great Passover Sabbath (Saturday), was past. They rolled a great stone before the doorway. Afterward the Chief Priests sent a guard to the sepulchre, to seal the stone and to watch, lest the disciples, taking His body away, might claim that He had risen from the dead.

REVIEW.

For what purpose did the Son of God come into this world? John 12: 27, 33. Rom. 6: 23. I. Tim. 1: 15.
On the Sunday before the Passover, what took place? Ps. 24: 7—10. Zech. 9: 9.
Can you tell why the Jews kept the Passover? Less. 14.
Describe what Jesus did in the Temple.
What did Jesus during the week at Jerusalem?
How did the Priests plan to take Jesus?
What did Jesus on Thursday evening? St. John 6: 51.
What did He say?
To what garden did He go?
Where was it? Who came there?
How did Judas betray Jesus?
To how many Judges, or trials, was Jesus led?
What became of Judas?
Who gave consent at last to the death of Jesus?
Because of what claim?
Can you describe the death of Jesus?
Did any strange events take place at His death?
How did they care for His body after death?
Who watched His tomb?
Where was He buried?

Notes. PASSION, endurance. SUFFERINGS, pains, or distresses felt. TRIUMPHANTLY, like a conqueror. STREWED, scattered about. OXEN, ETC., animals sold for sacrifices. EXCHANGED. Foreign Jews and others, desiring to make an offering for the Temple, must do so only with Jewish coin. These men exchanged money at a small charge. ADVICE, counsel. BETRAY, be an enemy, though seemingly a friend. HUMILITY, lowliness of mind. WASHING THE FEET, cooling and cleansing the travel-weary feet of another was a very refreshing service, though a most lowly one. TRAITOR, one who proves false to a friend. BREAD, the unleavened wafer of the Passover. BODY, that which contains the Life. REMEMBRANCE, a reminder. CUP, the wine used at the Passover feast. NEW TESTAMENT, a new inheritance, or testifying of the Love of God. BLOOD, that which was shed in atonement; for the cleansing of sin. REMISSION, sending away. SUPPER **OF** LIFE, the holy Sacrament of the Altar, the Feast in which the believer receives life and salvation [Catechism Part V]. HYMN, a psalm, or Jewish song of praise. MOUNT OF OLIVES, a lofty hill East from Jerusalem where were gardens and olive-trees. HIGH-PRIEST, [Lesson 13, 15,] he who now possessed this honor claimed it for one year only; and had no true right to it. SANHEDRIM, the high Court of seventy Priests, Elders and wise men, sitting in a circle, presided over by the High Priest. PONTIUS PILATE, the Roman, governing in Caesar's name, over Jerusalem. HEROD, Herod Antipas, tetrarch of Galilee, who slew John the Baptist; [Lesson 29,] Luke 13: 32. 23: 7—11; son of that Herod who destroyed the children of Bethlehem [Lesson 30,] KING OF THE JEWS, that spiritual King that had been promised to the Jews. Ps. 24: 7. 110: 1. [Lesson 30,] SCOURGE, to whip with cords. CRUCIFIED, nailed to a cross to die. THIEVES, those who had stolen. They were punished in those days by death. ROBE, a cloak, or shawl. SCARLET, of a red color, such as Kings wore. CALVARY, [the rounded "place of a skull,"] a spot, outside the walls of the city, [Levit. 4,] where criminals were put to death [Golgotha]. CROSS, two posts, or timbers crossed on which the condemned man was nailed or tied, planted in the ground like a T, or an X. FORGIVE, pardon, take away ill will. RENT, torn [Lesson 15 and 27,]. EARTHQUAKE, a shaking of the ground. PIERCED, thrust through [as with a spear]. BLOOD AND WATER, a proof that both the pericardium and the heart itself were wounded. SEPULCHRE, a cave, or room cut in the rocks, and used for burial. A stone rolled at the doorway was sealed with clay. SEAL, to fasten clay, or mortar between the door and tomb, so that no unnoticed person could disturb the tomb without leaving proof of the act.

Lesson 36.—The Sixth Sunday after Trinity.

RESURRECTION.

THE RISING OF JESUS FROM DEATH.

COMMIT JOHN 14: 19. I. COR. 15: 20, 21. READ MATT. 28: 1—15. MARK 16: 1—13. LUKE 24: 1—49. JOHN 20: 1—23.

THE STORY.

The next day after that on which Jesus died was the great Passover Sabbath. So the good women Mary of Magdala, (called the "Magdalena",) Joanna, Mary, Salome and others, after having bought fragrant spices, waited till the holy day was past; and then, very early, even before the dawn of Sunday, they went forth from the city to prepare the Lord's body for its true burial by wrapping spices about it with linen. On the way to the sepulchre, the women reasoned how they might roll aside that great stone, which Mary Magdalene and the other Mary had seen the men roll before the door.

But they did not know that a glorious angel of the LORD, whose face was like lightning, had come down from heaven and rolled back the stone, while the watchers trembled and sank down to the earth for fear; then fled to the city and told the Chief Priests what they had seen. The Chief Priests bribed the watchers to say that the disciples had stolen away the body of Jesus while they slept.

At sunrise the pious women stood at the sepulchre and saw that some one had rolled aside the stone. Mary Magdalene, thinking that the Lord's body had been carried away, ran to tell Peter and John of this, while the other women waited at the empty tomb.

Meanwhile, they enter and find, not the body of Jesus, but two bright angels who say to the frightened women "Fear not." "Ye seek Jesus of Nazareth which was crucified; He is risen,

The Women at the Sepulchre.

He is not here. "See the place where He lay," and "tell His disciples to go unto Galilee." "There shall ye see Him."

With great fear and joy they now also ran to tell the disciples the good news of their Master having risen from the dead.

Hearing the news, Peter and John came running to the sepulchre, and entering saw the linen of our Lord's burial laid in order. And they believed and departed wondering. Once more Mary Magdalene drew near to the sepulchre; when she also beheld two angels, and soon after a person, Whom she supposed to be the gardener, Who said: "Whom seekest thou?" Weeping, she said: "They have taken away my Lord and I know not where they have laid Him." She begged to know, if He had taken the Body, and where it was, that she might find it and lay it gently away. It was Jesus Who spoke, and He now called her by name "Mary"!

Then she knew Jesus and cried with joy "My Master!"

Some of the women, going to tell the disciples of the angels, also met our risen Saviour, Who saluted them, saying, "All hail"!

But when they told these things to the disciples all seemed to them as idle tales. They believed them not. But Peter also saw Him.

That same day, as two of the disciples sadly left Jerusalem for Emmaus, they were overtaken on the way by the Lord. They knew Him not. He talked, walked, reasoned, and at the village sat down with them; then they knew Him just as He was breaking the bread of the Supper. As they knew Him, He vanished, and when they, hastening back to the place in Jerusalem, where the disciples were very secretly gathered, declared that Jesus was indeed risen from the dead, Jesus Himself stood in their midst and said to all: "Peace be unto you." He breathed on them and said: "Receive ye the Holy Ghost." "As My Father hath sent Me, even so send I you." The disciples rejoiced together. Now they had indeed seen the risen Lord; and they knew that He had power over death as well as over life; and could raise up all the dead, at the last day, to judge them for the deeds done in the body. They were justified in believing in One Who could rise from the dead.

REVIEW.

On the Friday before what great day was Jesus crucified?
What did good women buy?
Can you name some of them?
Why did they wait?
How early did they begin their work of burial of the Lord's body?
Of what did they speak on their way to the sepulchre?
But of what vision did they not know?
How did the watching soldiers behave when the angel came?
Tell me the appearance of the angel.

What did the Chief Priests command and pay the soldiers to say?
Could they have seen all this while asleep?
What commands of God were therefore broken? 8th and 10th.
At sunrise of Sunday, what did the pious women find?
Who at once ran to tell Peter and John?
As the others enter the sepulchre, do they find the body of Jesus?
But whom do they see?
Did the angels tell them a glad message?
Tell me what it was.
What did the women now do?
What did Peter and John find when they came?
Did they believe that Jesus was risen?
How did they depart?
Who came again to the sepulchre?
Whom did she see? And what did she suppose?
Did the Man ask anything? How did she answer?
For what did she beg? Who was it Who spoke?
Did Mary at once know Jesus?
What did she call Him?
Who first therefore saw Jesus after He was risen from the dead?
Who also met Jesus? How did He salute them?
How did the disciples receive the glad news?
Who also saw Him?
Can you relate how, on that same day, the Lord appeared to two disciples?
As soon as they knew Him what did they do?
How did they find the other disciples? Why?
As the disciples spoke of Jesus' Resurrection, Who appeared among them? What did He say?
Tell what great gifts of power they were to receive?
What great mission were they to fulfill?
How did the sight of the Lord affect the disciples?
What great facts does His Resurrection prove?

Notes. SATURDAY, the seventh day of the week, the Jewish Sabbath or day of rest. MAGDALA, a town on the West shore of the Sea of Galilee. SPICES, herbs and gums, such as aloes and myrrh. St. John 19: 39. SUNDAY, the first day of the week, dedicated by heathens to the worship of the Sun; but kept by the Christians as the Lord's day for worship, instruction and rest. BURIAL, the Jews wrapped the body of the dead in linen, laying spices etc. in the folds, then placed the enfolded body in a rock-cut-sepulchre or tomb. REASONED, consulted together. TREMBLED, quaked with nervous fear. WATCHERS, guards. [It was death to a Roman sentinel to be found negligent of duty, or sleeping at his post.] EMPTY, not containing anything. FRIGHTENED, made to fear, or be dismayed. GARDENER, one having the care of a small piece of ground. BEGGED, humbly asked. "ALL HAIL," a salutation meaning "Rejoice". OVERTAKEN, caught up to, in the way, by another. EMMAUS, a small village of Judea, probably 7½ miles N. W. from Jerusalem. VANISHED, disappeared from sight. HASTENING, ever hurrying with new zeal. SECRETLY, in quiet, at time or place unknown by others. HOLY GHOST, the Comforter, the Third Person of the adorable Holy Trinity. REJOICED, were exceedingly glad.

Lesson 37.—The Seventh Sunday after Trinity.

ASCENSION.

THE DEPARTURE OF JESUS.

COMMIT PHILIPPIANS 2: 9—11. READ MATT. 28: 18—20. MARK 16: 19—20. LUKE 24: 44—53. JOHN 20: 30—31. ACTS 1: 3—12.

THE STORY.

Our blessed Redeemer and Lord, Jesus Christ, often showed Himself alive to His disciples after His rising from the dead. He appeared to seven while they were fishing in the Sea of Galilee, and He also met them on a mountain of Galilee as He had appointed.

He remained visibly on earth among men for forty days. He gave the apostles authority to go in His Name and teach all who would hear and learn to believe in Jesus. They were therefore to baptize the people in the name of the Father, and of the Son, and of the Holy Ghost, as a proof of faith in the heart and of God's welcome of believing penitents into the Church.

And He opened their minds to understand how the Law of Moses, the words of the Prophets and the Psalms were written chiefly to foretell Him, Jesus the Saviour of men.

Once more He met them at Jerusalem and commanded them not to depart from that city, until the promised "Comforter," the Holy Spirit sent by the Father should come unto them with power from on high. Then they would become witnesses for the Lord Jesus in Judea and in Samaria and to the utmost parts of the earth.

Jesus at length led His disciples out from the city as far as to Bethany. Here, while they looked upon Him lifting up His Hands as a priest to bless them, He was Himself lifted up and parted from them, going into heaven, and a cloud hid His disappearing Form from their last steadfast look.

But when their glances fell to the earth, lo! beside them stood two angels, who said: "Men of Galilee, why stand ye, gazing up into heaven? This same Jesus, Who is taken up from you into heaven, shall so come in like manner, as ye have seen Him go into heaven."

Glad because they had been permitted to see the ascension of their Lord, our Saviour, the disciples came back to Jerusalem and were daily found in the Temple, worshipping God and preaching of Jesus the Christ, Whom they had known, loved and seen at last go up to heaven, to sit in glory with the Father forever; to plead for all those sinners who repent and call upon Him and to prepare a home for all who are saved by His power and mercy.

REVIEW.

Did Jesus ever show Himself living after the day of His rising from the dead? To whom?
How did He appear to seven of them?
Again where did He meet them?
Had He promised this?
How long did He visibly remain on earth after His resurrection?
What authority did He give to the apostles?
Of what were they to teach the world?
Also, what sacramental act were they to perform? Matt. 28: 19.
What is Baptism?
Of what is Baptism a sign?
Into what does it welcome us?
In Whose Name is it done?
How did the Lord help the minds of His disciples?
For what were the Law, Prophecies and Psalms chiefly written?
What glorious title do we give to Jesus?
Did He die to save all or only a few? John 3: 16.
Where did He once more meet them?
And what did He command?
Who would come unto them?
What would He bring unto them?
What would they then become?
How far would they bear their witness of Jesus?
To what little town did Jesus at length lead His disciples?
What took place there? Into what place was He going?
What caused Him to be seen no more?
Who however stood by the disciples as they gazed?
What did these messengers say?
What is an angel? Heb. 1: 14.
What glorious promise did they give?
Will the same Jesus ever come again?
Why were the disciples glad?
To what city did they return?
In what place were they daily found?
How were they occupied?
Why did they preach about Jesus? I. John 1: 1—3.

Why had Jesus gone to heaven? John 20: 17.
What will Jesus do for those sinners who repent and call upon Him? Rom. 8: 34. I. John 2: 1.
Is there a place in heaven for you? John 14: 2.
By Whose power and mercy alone can we be saved?

Notes. ASCENSION, the going up of Jesus to heaven, exaltation. REDEEMER, He Who brought us into forgiveness and salvation, by paying His innocent sufferings and death. APPOINTED, set to do a certain work. VISIBLY, in a way that can be seen. BAPTIZE, faithfully and officially to apply water to a believer in the Name of the Holy Trinity. [See Luther's Catechism, Part IV. the Sacrament of Regeneration]. COMFORTER, One who supplies relief. WITNESSES, those who speak of what they have seen or known. JUDEA, the Southern part of Palestine in the time of our Lord, the country around and South of Jerusalem, abounding in hills and valleys, plains and wilderness. BETHANY, a village probably 15 furlongs East of Jerusalem situated on the Mount of Olives. DISAPPEARING, passing out of sight, vanishing. STEADFAST, fixed, constant. GLANCES, looks, glimpses, sight. MEN OF GALILEE, the disciples were nearly all from Galilee, [fishermen etc.] the Northern district of the Holy Land. GAZING, steadily looking. PREACHING, proclaiming, teaching. LOVED, admired.

Lesson 38.—The Eighth Sunday after Trinity.

A LESSON IN REVIEW.

COMMIT II. PETER 3: 18. READ MATT. 9: 25. 27. ACTS 1: 1—12. ROMANS 8.

THE STORY.

The sinful Jews were carried captive to Babylon. Some, like Mordecai, Daniel and Ezekiel never returned. Esther, Mordecai's fair cousin, became Queen of Babylon, and saved her people from threatened destruction. During the seventy years of the Babylonian Captivity (B. C. 606–536), and after the return of many to Jerusalem and Judea, prophets arose and spoke of the Coming One, Jesus the Messiah, and all the holy Types; officers, persons, places, things, reminded the people of Him.

Solomon's great Temple, which took the place of the Tabernacle, and which was destroyed by Nebuchadnezzar, was rebuilt by Zerubbabel. King Herod afterward repaired it. Hence it is called "the latter Temple." It was burnt by the Roman general Titus A. D. 70.

The Jews obeyed their own princes or at times foreign

masters from the return to the Holy City, until at Bethlehem the Babe JESUS was born of the virgin Mary. Shepherds of Judea and Magi from the far East came to worship the new born King. Herod sought to kill the Child. Joseph and Mary took the Infant to Egypt lest Herod should find and slay Him. Afterward they returned to Nazareth and piously attended the yearly Passover at Jerusalem, taking the child Jesus at His twelfth year to be received into the fellowship of the Jewish congregation. Here He was lost by His parents three days, but found in the Temple among the doctors of the Law.

Jesus the Lord grew to become a holy man. Before He began His work of teaching and saving, God sent a faithful forerunner John the Baptist, who led the people to repent and confess how greatly they needed a Saviour.

Then Jesus, the Son of God and son of man, came and was also baptized by John, while the blessing of God the Father and the Holy Spirit descended upon Him.

Not long after, John was slain by wicked King Herod.

Jesus now began to teach the people, by parables, (as the sower, the lost sheep, the prodigal son etc.) of Himself and of His Kingdom; and showed, by working great miracles, (healing the sick, blind, deaf, lame, raising the dead etc.) that He truly was God in man. He did many wonderful works, manifested His glory by His Transfiguration, gathered many disciples, whom He made His followers (the Church), and sent forth twelve of them with power as apostles, to teach their fellow-men of Him. At last, after triumphantly entering Jerusalem (yet in a lowly way), and instituting the Holy Supper of His Body and His Blood, He was seized by the Jews and Romans and after a forced trial, crowned with thorns and crucified because He said He was "JESUS OF NAZARETH THE KING OF THE JEWS," as the writing put upon His cross declared.

But the dear Saviour suffered death for us, and paid the debt we owed to God on account of our sins.

So, after He lay in the tomb,—on the third day He rose from the dead: for forty days often stood visibly among His disciples; then blessed them and went to Heaven, to sit as Judge of the quick and the dead, with the Father in glory everlasting.

He shall come again from thence to receive all the true church unto Himself and to separate forever the wicked and the good.

REVIEW.

A sad fate fell upon the Jews, what was it? Did they return? Mention some who did not.
Tell of Esther, and how she saved the Jews?
Of Whom did the Prophets speak?
What are Types? Of Whom do they remind us?
Tell what happened to the Temples of Israel. Haggai 2: 9.
How long was it from the return of the children of Judah till the Birth of Jesus?
Where was Jesus born? Who was His mother?
Who came to see and worship Him?
Who sought to slay Jesus?
In what places did Jesus live?
What befell Him once in Jerusalem?
Who was Jesus' fore-runner?
What did He to Jesus?
Is it needful now to repent of sins? Acts 2: 38.
Can you tell anything of the wonderful life of Jesus? Matt. 17: 5, 12.
What is a parable? Mention one.
What is a miracle? Mention one.
What were His followers called?
What do His followers constitute?
What great Supper did our Lord establish?
How did He die?
What great event took place after His death and burial?
Why did Jesus die?
What accusation was nailed with Him on the cross?
Did the disciples see Him after His rising from death?
What did they lastly see Him do?
Why will Jesus come again?

Notes. QUEEN, the highest female ruler in a kingdom, wife or widow of the King THREATENED, promised as punishment, or danger. MESSIAH, the Hebrew word for Christ, or "the Anointed." A. D., an abbreviation for "Anno Domini," Latin for "In the year of the Lord." FOREIGN, of a different nation. PRINCES, chief rulers. MAGI, wise and holy men, probably from Persia, priests. HEROD, the Herod who slew John the Baptist was called Herod Antipas, he was son of Herod the King of Judea at Christ's Birth, and was tetrarch of Galilee. He was a cruel and immoral man. SAFETY, the condition of being free from all danger. DOCTORS, old teachers, or scribes well versed in the law of Moses. SAVING, taking from harm or destruction. FORE-RUNNER, a messenger, going on before to announce the coming of a King. CONFESS, speak out the truth. HOLY SUPPER, "the New Testament Passover-Feast." The Sacrament of Strengthening. Catechism Part V. FORCED, unjustly compelled, or unwillingly impelled, in a constrained or unfair way. QUICK, those now living. I, N. R. I., the initials of the Roman writing on the cross; (I)esus (N)azarenus (R)ex (I)udaeorum, "Jesus the Nazarene King of the Jews." See picture on page 111.

Lesson 39.—The Ninth Sunday after Trinity.

THE COMING OF THE HOLY SPIRIT.

COMMIT I. CORINTHIANS 12: 3, 4.   READ JOEL 2: 28.   JOHN 15: 26, 27. 16: 7—14.   20: 21—23.   ACTS 1: 4—8.   2: 1—47.

THE STORY.

The Third Person of the Holy Trinity is the HOLY GHOST. When Jesus went away from His disciples into heaven, He promised that the Holy Ghost, (or Spirit) would soon come to

The Outpouring of the Holy Ghost.

them, while they tarried in Jerusalem. He spoke of the Holy Spirit as the "Comforter" and the "Spirit of truth."

At the Baptism of Jesus, the Spirit had appeared in the form of a Dove. He would come to the disciples to strengthen their faith in the truth, and help them bravely to teach of Christ to all men. It is the Spirit Who convinces us of our sin, leads us to Christ and puts into our hearts the power of Christ; so that, at the day of judgment, we may be saved, when Satan and all the ungodly shall be cast out, to die forever.

The Lord gave the disciples authority to speak of God's warnings and punishments, and of His promises and rewards. This is sometimes called the "Power of the Keys." But God alone can punish, or reward forever.

At Pentecost, according to Jesus' promise, the disciples were filled with the power of the Holy Ghost. They were in Jerusalem, ten days after Jesus ascended; and, as they sat together, there came to them a sound as of a rushing wind; while divided flames, like fire, appeared and settled down upon each one. They were all inspired with new courage and every disciple began to speak in a new language, as the Spirit gave him power.

When the multitude of Jews heard this, they were much surprised, and tried in vain to explain it. This was the act of God, as Joel the prophet had said.

Then Peter and the other apostles boldly stood up and spoke to all men of this strange thing, and of Jesus, Whom the Jews had wickedly crucified; but Whom God had raised up, and Who, being the Son of God in man, had ascended to heaven.

Many, hearing these words, asked what they should do. Peter said: "Repent, every one, and be baptized in the Name of Jesus Christ." Then about three thousand believing souls were added to the disciples.

REVIEW.

Name the Third Person in the Holy Trinity?
Whom had Jesus promised to send to the disciples?
Did Jesus give Him two beautiful names?
Had the Spirit appeared before?
For what would the Spirit come?
What is the work of the Holy Spirit?
Tell what is the object of the Holy Spirit's work? I. John 5: 11, 12.
What authority was given to the disciples?
Has this power a name? Matt. 16: 19. See Catechism.
But Who can alone open or close heaven by forgiving or retaining sins? Matt. 9: 6. Mark 2: 7.
A great event took place at Pentecost, what was it?
Can you describe the event? II. Peter 1: 21.

By what was each soul filled?
How did each disciple show the power of God?
Did this surprise the Jews?
Did they try to explain the matter?
But Whose act was this?
Which prophet had said so? Joel 2: 28, 29.
And what did Peter and the rest do?
To whom did he speak? About what?
Had the Jews done wrong to Jesus?
How did God overcome the evil work with good?
Where was Jesus now?
How long after His resurrection did He ascend to heaven?
How long after His ascension did the Holy Ghost fill the souls of the apostles and others?
How long after Easter is Pentecost?
How did this affect many?
What great duty did Peter urge?
Can you tell me what it is to repent?
What is Baptism?
How many believers were added that day to the Church?

Notes. STRENGTHEN, to make more powerful. CONVINCES, proves very clearly JUDGMENT DAY, the day, when, at the end of the world, Christ will separate the believers from the wicked. Matt. 16: 27. 25: 31. Mark 6: 11. 8: 38. Acts 1: 11. II. Thes. 1: 7, 8. II. Peter 2: 9. 3: 7. AUTHORITY, the right to act in the name of another. POWER OF THE KEYS, the power to open for, or close from men the door of blessings of the visible Church. PENTECOST, the fiftieth day after the Passover, celebrated as the festival of the giving of the Law to Moses, and the living in tabernacles [tents], in the Wilderness. It is sometimes called the feast of [7] weeks. In honor of the Coming of the Holy Ghost it is called by Christians, Whitsunday, [i. e. Whitsunday, white being the emblem of purification.] INSPIRED, moved by the Spirit of God to act, or speak. COURAGE, bravery, absence of fear. POWER, ability to do, or endure. AMAZED, very greatly surprised, filled with wonder. BOLDLY, in a daring manner.

Lesson 40.—The Tenth Sunday after Trinity.

PERSECUTION AND IMPRISONMENT.

COMMIT I. CORINTHIANS 15: 57, 58.   READ ACTS 4 AND 5.

THE STORY.

The Priests and other Jewish leaders were offended at the apostles' teaching about Jesus and His Resurrection. They talked with the Captain of the Temple, who made Peter and John their prisoners. The next day, when the Priests and rulers were gathered in the great Council, Peter and John were brought to them for trial.

The Council asked the apostles by what right they preached and healed the sick; (for God gave them power to perform many miracles in Jesus' Name.) Peter said that it was by the command and Name of Jesus Christ that all these things were done. The Stone, which the builders (Jews) refused, was the chief of the Church. Not Peter, but Christ is the Head of the Church. We can be saved only in Jesus.

The Council dared not punish the good apostles, but could only warn them and forbid them to teach the people the Name of Jesus. But Peter said we *must* speak of Jesus, Who was so wonderful.

They went away, praising God that they were safe; continued their good work of preaching and doing marvellous miracles; and great numbers of the sick were healed. Multitudes of believers were added to the Church.

The angry High Priest and those with him now sent and again made the apostles prisoners. But that night the angel of the Lord opened the prison, brought the innocent apostles forth and said: "Go speak again in the Temple of salvation in Jesus."

Next morning the Council sent to the prison for their captives. But though the prison was shut the apostles were gone.

Soon word came to the High Priest and the Captain that the apostles were again preaching in the Temple. Again therefore they were seized and taken to the High Priest. Then Peter said: "We ought to obey God rather than men, and we must bear witness of Jesus."

Now there was in the Council an old teacher, named Gamaliel. This wise and well known doctor stood up and warned the Jews, saying: If this is only man's work, done by these men it will come to nothing; but if this work of the apostles be of God, you cannot overcome it. Let them alone. To fight against God is no gain to man.

Calling the apostles, they beat them, forbade them once more to teach the rejected Name of Jesus and again let them go. The apostles departed, glad that they were counted worthy to suffer shame for Jesus' sake. So, daily, in every place, they taught their fellow men of the holy Saviour.

REVIEW.

At what were the Jewish leaders offended?
How did they show their enmity?
To what great meeting were the apostles brought?
About what were they examined?
Had God given them great power?
In Whose name were all their good works done?
To what is Jesus beautifully likened?
What comparison did Peter make between the Church and a building?
Is Peter the Head of the Church?
But Who alone can be?
Can we be saved by any other Name than that of Jesus?
In what way did the Council act in this matter?
How did Peter reply?
Did they continue to teach and heal the people?
Were many led to believe in Christ?
What did the angry rulers do? Who visited the prison?
How did the angel wonderfully help the apostles?
What did he command?
For whom did the Jews send to the prison on the next day?
Did they find them there? Tell where the apostles were.
Whose command were they obeying?
Were the apostles again seized?
How did Peter explain his duty?
Who was in the Council? What did he say?
What did the Council then do?
How did the apostles depart?
Did they neglect their holy duty?
Were the apostles glad only because they were free, or rather because they were permitted to serve and suffer for Jesus' sake?

Notes. OFFENDED, displeased, affronted. COUNCIL, the sacred Sanhedrim, composed of 70 High Priests, Elders and Scribes. It was the highest court of the Jews. REJECTED, cast aside. SHAME, disgrace.

Lesson 41.—The Eleventh Sunday after Trinity.

THE DEACONS, STEPHEN AND THE PERSECUTION.

COMMIT ROMANS 12: 11—14. READ ACTS 6 TO 8: 4

THE STORY.

Matthias, a pious disciple was given, by lot, the place of the traitor Judas. The Church at Jerusalem was now grown large and strong. There was a general distribution daily, from a common fund, to all the poor. Some of the Grecian widows were neglected and not cared for. And the apostles soon found that they could not properly attend to the public preaching of the gospel and prayer and to the supply of food to the poor.

They now called the Church together and suggested that seven honest and holy men should be chosen to attend to the business of caring for the poor.

These men being selected were called *"Deacons"*; and were set apart, as officers to care for the work of the Church, with prayer and the laying on of the apostles' hands.

Among the seven Deacons Stephen was the most distinguished. He not only zealously cared for the poor and sick, but was full of faith and power; so that he wrought great miracles among the people.

But Stephen was caught by the Jews and carried away to the Council. Here he earnestly spoke to all concerning Christ and cried out that he saw a vision of heaven and Jesus. Then the cruel Jews ran upon him, led him out of the city and killed him by casting stones upon him. As he was first to die for Christ he is called the first "martyr". Poor, forgiving Stephen as he died, prayed "Lord, lay not this sin to their charge." Among those who stood by, and saw this riotous act, was a young man named Saul. Pious men carried Stephen to his burial and greatly mourned for him.

The persecution now became greater. The Church at Jerusalem was scattered abroad. Philip, of the Deacons, went preaching of Christ to the city of Samaria. The people gladly heard him because of the miracles which he did. At last Samaria was ready to believe in Jesus.

Saul made great trouble in Jerusalem, going everywhere and committing to prison every one whom he found believing in Jesus Christ.

REVIEW.

Do you remember what became of Judas Iscariot? Less. 35.
Who filled his place among the twelve apostles?
Had the Church prospered?
What good work was done daily?
But did any neglect occur?
Could the apostles do fully all the work that they had to do?
How did they propose to arrange the difficulty?

Tell what was done.
What were the selected men called?
How many were they?
How were they ordained, or appointed?
Of the deacons who seems to be the foremost?
How was he useful?
Did trouble befall him? How?
Before whom was he taken? Less. 35 and 40.
Tell what took place in the Council.
How did they treat poor Stephen at last? 5th Com.
Mention the title now given to him.
What was his last act? Was not this like Jesus?
For whom did he pray? Matt. 5: 43, 44.
Who witnessed Stephen's death?
How was Stephen buried?
Can you tell what great trouble now arose?
Had it any effect upon the Church in the holy city?
To whom did Philip go?
How was he received? And why?
Had Samaria before refused the gospel of Jesus? Less. 32.
Saul was making trouble; how did he do it?

Notes. DEACONS, those Church-officers who care for the material welfare of the congregation, — the house, the sick, the poor, the repairs, the finances etc. DISTRIBUTION, sharing among many. SUPPLY, a quantity of good things contributed and collected by the Church, to be given to the needy. GRECIAN, those Jews who had come from Asia Minor and spoke the Greek language. NEGLECTED, overlooked, forgotten. SUGGESTED, proposed. HONEST, true in dealing. SELECTED, chosen. "LAYING ON OF HANDS," the holy act of the apostles, ratifying the election of the deacons. DISTINGUISHED, noted, foremost, spoken of and pointed out. ZEALOUSLY, earnestly. MARTYR, one who holds to the truth and dies for it.

Lesson 42.—The twelfth Sunday after Trinity.

PHILIP TEACHING SAMARIA AND THE EUNUCH.

COMMIT ROMANS 6: 17, 18. READ ACTS 8: 4—40. ST. MATTHEW 10: 5—7. ST. JOHN 4: 1—42.

THE STORY.

While the wicked Jews were bitterly persecuting the Church at Jerusalem and Saul was bringing the pious followers of Jesus, both men and women, to prison; the pious Deacon Philip went to Samaria. Although, during our Saviour's life, the Samaritans were not ready to receive Jesus; they at length learned to know and love Him Who is our best Friend on earth. The work of Philip filled the city with joy for he healed many that were sick.

Now Simon the Sorcerer, (a magician, in whose deceptions the Samaritans had before trusted for healing,) saw Philip as he taught of Christ and performed many miracles; came, believing in Christ, and was baptized by Philip. Peter and John, hearing of the Deacon's success, also came to Samaria and prayed for the people. They laid their hands on the people and they

Philip and the Eunuch.

received the Holy Spirit. When Simon the Sorcerer saw this he came with money in his hand to buy the power of God so as to work miracles also.

Peter and John rebuked him and taught him to repent; for such things are not bought with money. They are the *gift* of God.

Philip was now commanded by the angel of the Lord to go toward Gaza. It was a desert road; but as he went, he overtook the chariot of a Eunuch, a man of great authority under Candace, the Queen of Ethiopia.

The officer was returning from worship in Jerusalem and reading the Book of the Prophet Isaiah. When he had run quickly to the chariot Philip said, "Understandest thou what thou readest?" The Eunuch invited him to come up, sit with him in the chariot and explain what he had read from the 7th and 8th verses of the 53rd chapter. Then Philip taught the Eunuch of the sufferings and death of our Lord and Saviour Jesus Christ, in Whose Name all should be baptized.

As they came to a little stream, the Eunuch said, "See! here is water; should not I be baptized?" Philip answered, "If thou believest with all thine heart thou mayest be baptized." The officer answered, "I believe that Jesus Christ is the Son of God."

Then Philip baptized him and departed. The officer rejoiced on his homeward way; while Philip beginning at Azotus went preaching from city to city for 53 miles till he came to Caesarea. Here Philip remained a long time.

REVIEW.

How were the Jews dealing with the Church at Jerusalem?
Did Saul do any harm?
To whom did Philip go?
What office had Philip?
Had the Samaritans received Jesus? See Less. 32. Matt. 10: 5. Luke 9: 52—54.
Why not?
Had they now learned to know Him?
Tell me Who Jesus is.
How were the Samaritans satisfied with Philip's teaching? Why?
Tell who Simon was in that city.
Describe a sorcerer.
Had the Samaritans thought him true?
Did even Simon believe Philip?
Did he perform, as a sign of his faith, any holy act?
Is not Baptism a necessary act? St. Mark 16: 16. Acts 2: 38. 10: 47.
Who now came down to Samaria?
What great power was received by the Samaritans?
What did Simon the sorcerer think and do?
How did Peter and John teach the magician?
Can we buy anything from God?
By Whose precious blood have we all been bought? I. Cor. 6: 20. 7: 23.

How was Philip now commanded?
Whom did the obedient Deacon meet?
Should we shirk hard duties?
In what was the stranger engaged?
Can you repeat what he was reading?   Is. 53: 7, 8.   Acts 8: 32, 33.
What did Philip ask?
Did the Eunuch invite him to ride with him?
Could Philip explain the Prophet's words?
About Whom were they written?
Can you explain them?
What did they tell of Jesus?
To what while riding did they come?
For what did the Eunuch ask?
How did Philip answer?
Did the Eunuch make a good confession?   Matt. 10: 32.   Rom. 10: 9, 10.
And did Philip then baptize the Eunuch?
In what mind did the Eunuch continue his journey?
Tell what Philip now did.
In what city did he long remain?   Acts 21: 8.
Should you believe in Jesus with all your heart, and say so?
May we not all be missionaries for Christ?

Notes. EUNUCH, a chamberlain, or other high officer of state. BITTERLY, with fierce and cruel earnestness. DEACON, these officers though only appointed for the care of temporal things, were useful also as evangelists, or missionaries in the days of persecution; and were permitted to baptize. SORCERER, a magician, one who claimed to have power from God to do wonders. DECEPTION, making the false seem true. TRUSTED, depended upon, put confidence in. GAZA, the Philistine city, near Egypt, whose gates Samson [Lesson 17] carried away.   Judg. 16: 3.   DESERT, a waste, unused land; usually sandy, rocky, and barren. CANDACE, the title "Queen" in Ethiopia. ETHIOPIA, that part of Africa south of Egypt. AZOTUS, [Ashdod,] a town of Philistia near the Great Sea. CÆSAREA, Herod's chief city on the Great Sea; named after the Emperor Cæsar.

Lesson 43.—The Thirteenth Sunday after Trinity.

THE GREAT CHANGE IN SAUL.

COMMIT II. CORINTHIANS 12: 9.   READ ACTS 9: 1—31.   22: 1—22.
26: 1—21.

THE STORY.

The young man, whom we found standing by at Stephen's death, was Saul; one of the most active and cruel enemies of the Church of Jesus. He was born at Tarsus in Cilicia, and came to Jerusalem to sit at Gamaliel's feet, to learn the Jewish law. He grew up a very strict Pharisee. It happened that Saul's Jewish family had also the great honor and privilege of being

The Great Change in Saul. 133

called "Roman citizens." This was a protection to Saul; for no man dared to treat a Roman citizen unjustly.

But Saul was blindly trying to fight against the Lord. He thought that the Jews were right and the religion of Jesus was false. So he persecuted the Church at Jerusalem; and having scattered the believers there, he set out for Damascus with letters from the High Priest to the Governor, to take and bring back bound to Jerusalem those who had fled from that city.

Saul, the Persecutor.

As young Saul with his men was nearing the city of Damascus, a sudden glorious light shone from heaven upon him. As he fell to the ground he heard a Voice, which said: "Saul! Saul! Why persecutest thou Me?" "I am Jesus." "Arise, go into the city and it shall be told thee what thou must do."

Saul arose. Those around him were silent. They had heard a voice but seen no man. Saul, amazed and trembling, found that he was blind! They led him now, humbled and penitent, into Damascus, quite changed from his persecuting spirit into one of humility.

Here, in the street called "Straight", he lodged in great remorse for three days at the house of Justus.

At Damascus lived an old disciple, Ananias, whom the Lord in a vision now sent to Saul; and foretold that he who before had persecuted the Church of Christ, would in later days be a fearless defender and missionary of the truth. He would in fact suffer much in the cause of Christ.

Ananias bravely went in and comforted Saul, by power from God healed his blind eyes and baptized him. Soon Saul was strong in faith. He read and understood the Scriptures. As soon as possible he began to teach in the Synagogue, proving to the amazed Jews that Jesus was indeed the Son of God.

The Jews at once became his enemies, tried to kill him, and watched at the gates of the city day and night, lest he should escape. But the disciples let him down by a basket and rope from a window in the wall of the city. Thus he escaped and came back to Jerusalem. Here the disciples feared him as a secret foe. At last Barnabas, a true disciple, took him by the hand and brought him to the apostles. He spoke so boldly in Jerusalem of Jesus our blessed Saviour, that the Grecian Jews were ready to slay him. Then the disciples brought him down to Cæsarea and sent Saul to Tarsus his birthplace.

REVIEW.

At what evil work do we first find Saul?
Describe his character.
At what place was he born?
For what did he come to Jerusalem?
Who was his teacher? Acts 22: 3. Less. 40.
Of what Jewish sect was he a member?
Tell what great honor was enjoyed by Saul's family.
Why was this an advantage to Saul? Acts 22: 25—28.
In what was Saul blindly engaged?
Was he in earnest however?
Did he suppose that he was doing wrong?
To what city did he go? For what purpose?
Near Damascus what strange event happened to him?
Describe the circumstance.
What did he see? Who spoke?
Did Saul find now that he had been doing evil?

How was he affected when he found his mistake?
Did the light affect Saul's eyes?
To whose house did his companions lead him?
How long did he lodge there in sorrow?
Did the Lord send any one to Saul?
What did He foretell about Saul?
Did Ananias bravely go and comfort Saul?
How did he help Saul?
Soon what do we find Saul doing?
What did he prove? Did this surprise the Jews?
Why must Saul leave Damascus?
How did he escape? II Cor. 11: 32, 33.
To what city did he come?
Among the disciples there, who was his first friend?
Did Saul speak boldly for Jesus even in Jerusalem?
Did this prove dangerous?
Then what did the disciples do with Saul? Acts 21: 39.
May not any one repent and believe in Jesus? John 3: 16.

Notes. CHANGE, a difference in life made by new motives or principles. TARSUS, the chief city of Cilicia, famous for its learning. CILICIA, a fertile and populous country, in the S. E. part of Asia Minor. PHARISEE, one of that sect of Jews, distinguished for the strict observance of all outward religious duty. PRIVILEGE, a favor enjoyed by but one or a few. ROMAN, pertaining to the city, or government of Rome; at that time the chief city of the known world. CITIZEN, one who enjoys the rights and liberties of a city. UNJUSTLY, without right, or fairness. DAMASCUS, the chief city of Syria, one of the oldest in the world. SILENT, speechless. REMORSE, regret and despair. MISSIONARY, one who preaches of Christ to the world in darkness. HEALED, restored to health. SYNAGOGUES, Jewish houses for public worship. ESCAPED, found deliverance or liberty.

Lesson 44.—The Fourteenth Sunday after Trinity.

THE JOURNEY OF PETER.

COMMIT ACTS 10: 34, 35. READ ACTS 9: 31—43. 10. 11: 1—18.

THE STORY.

Days of peace followed those of persecution and the Church grew. Peter went from place to place teaching, and strengthening the believers. At Lydda he found Æneas palsied. To him he said: "Æneas, Jesus Christ maketh thee whole." And he arose restored. Many seeing this believed in Jesus.

Now in Joppa, Dorcas, a pious woman and active in good works to the poor, grew sick and died. As Lydda was not far, the disciples at Joppa sent to Peter, begging him to come unto them at once. Peter came and saw the poor widows weeping for

Dorcas and showing the garments she had made for them. Peter kneeled down and prayed that her life might return. And the Lord gave back her life. Many therefore in Joppa turned to the Lord. Peter remained there for a time, by the sea; in the house of Simon, a tanner of Joppa.

Peter Preaching to Cornelius.

At Cæsarea meanwhile, a devout and benevolent centurion, Cornelius, of the Italian soldiers, saw an angel of the Lord, who said that God had heard his prayers and known his good deeds of kindness; and now commanded him to send men to Joppa, to Simon's house, inquiring for Peter who would come to Cornelius and teach him what he should do. Immediately Cornelius sent two of his household servants and a soldier to Joppa.

On the next day about the time that they arrived in Joppa, Peter went up to the house-top to pray. He became very hungry; and, while they prepared food in the house, Peter fell into a trance and three times saw a great sheet let down from heaven and full of all manner of wild beasts of the earth and creeping things. And he heard a voice saying: "Rise Peter, kill and eat." But Peter said: "Not so Lord, for I have never eaten anything common, or unclean." "What God hath

Peter's Miraculous Deliverance.

cleansed, that call not thou common", was the answer. While Peter thought on this vision, behold the men from Cornelius were knocking at the door and asking whether Peter lodged there. Peter went down to them and the servants of Cornelius told him their message. On the morrow Peter and six of the men of Joppa followed them to Cæsarea.

When they came to the house of Cornelius, they found that with the centurion many others were met to await them. As

Cornelius told his vision, Peter found that God was ready to accept common Gentiles and pious Jews alike as believers in Christ; and that whosoever would trust in Christ and live well should not perish, but be saved. Then Peter spoke to all these Gentiles of Christ Jesus our blessed and holy Saviour, and as he did so, the Holy Spirit came upon all his hearers. This showed that God had sent Peter's vision to teach that the Gentiles were also precious to God and if they repented and believed would be saved. After certain days Peter returned to Jerusalem, and told to all the Jewish disciples how God had broken away the wall of partition between Jews and Gentiles. The Gentiles were no longer despised by the Jewish disciples. Some time afterward Peter at Jerusalem was again released from prison by the angel of the Lord.

REVIEW.

Did the Church flourish during the days of peace?
In what was Peter engaged?
Coming to Lydda, whom did Peter find?
How did he help him? By Whose power was it?
Did good results follow?
How did faithful Dorcas prove that she was a true disciple? James 2: 14—19.
In what town did she die?
To whom did the disciples send?
Did Peter find that a pious woman was dead?
Did Peter do anything wonderful?
But could Peter have done this of himself?
Did this miracle cause much faith in Joppa?
Did Peter leave Joppa at once?
Why do we love the kind and good?
Where did Peter remain?
Describe Cornelius. In what city was he?
Had he a glorious vision from God?
Tell the angel's message to him.
Did the angel command Cornelius?
For whom should he send? Why?
Did Peter also see a vision? Describe how.
Where was Peter at the time?
Can you tell what the vision was?
How often did it appear?
What conversation took place?
Do you know why the Lord sent this vision?
Should Christians help each other?
Tell how Peter came and met Cornelius.

Of Whom did Peter speak?
Did any special event take place?
Since the Lord had blessed these Gentile believers, what holy sacramental act was necessary?
What is Baptism? Catech. Part IV.
Are all souls precious to God?
To what city did Peter return?
What did he tell the Jewish disciples?
How was Peter himself helped by an angel soon afterward?
Had he been so helped before?

Notes. PALSIED, made powerless in body. BENEVOLENT, kind in wishes and actions. CENTURION, a captain. ITALIAN BAND, Roman soldiers enlisted in Italy. HOUSETOP, the flat roof of the house, often used as a place of meditation or prayer. TRANCE, a state of mind, in which the world around us is forgotten;—a kind of dream. BEASTS, fourfooted walking animals. [The Jewish law did not permit certain animals to be eaten. Hence they were called "Unclean". Lev. 11: 2—8, 13—23.] AWAITED, expected to meet. ACCEPT, receive. GENTILES, all strangers, or foreigners who were not Jews. PERISH, die, be lost. PARTITION, a separation, a dividing, or bounding wall. JOPPA, [now Jaffa] a town by the Great [or Mediterranean] Sea, 35 m. S. of Cæsarea.

Lesson 45.—The Fifteenth Sunday after Trinity.

BARNABAS, PAUL AND MARK THE MISSIONARIES.

COMMIT ROMANS 1: 16, 17. READ ACTS 12: 24 TO 14: 28.

THE STORY.

Now at Antioch in Syria there were also some true men who had learned to believe in the Lord. Good Barnabas was sent from Jerusalem to teach them more fully of Jesus and our salvation; by His taking upon Himself our punishment, and thus purifying us for eternal life. This is called the "forgiveness of sins". Soon Barnabas went from Antioch to Tarsus to bring Saul (who was now called Paul), that he might help him to teach at Antioch. Paul came and remained with Barnabas a full year. The believers in Christ at Antioch were the first to be called "Christians".

A sad famine now befell Judea. So Barnabas and Paul were sent with gifts from the Church at Antioch to the poor brethren at Jerusalem.

Barnabas and Paul soon came back from Jerusalem, and, taking John Mark the son of Mary, sister of Barnabas; by the Lord's command started upon a long journey. They went from

Antioch to Seleucia; crossed the island of Cyprus, from which Barnabas had formerly come, and there taught of Jesus at Salamis. At Paphos Elymas the magician tried to oppose God's word, but was punished for a time with blindness. Timid John now forsook them and went back to Jerusalem.

The missionaries then sailed to Asia Minor and traveled to Perga, then to Antioch in Pisidia. Here the Jews rejected them.

Antioch in Syria, where Believers were first called Christians.

But when Paul stood up and spoke to the Gentiles, of the great promises of God fulfilled in Jesus, Who was crucified and rose again, they gladly believed. If we repent of our sins and come to Jesus in prayer we shall be forgiven.

The next place to which the servants of Christ came was Iconium, where they were persecuted. Barnabas and Paul now traveled to Derbe and Lystra; where the people seeing them heal a man born lame, thought that the heathen gods, Jupiter and

Mercury were come down to visit them, and would have made a sacrifice to them.

But the missionaries explained that they were only teachers of the good news about Jesus, and worked these miracles by His power.

At Lystra however, furious Jews from Antioch in Pisidia found them; and exciting an uproar, they persecuted the apostles. Paul was stoned, like Stephen, and drawn out of the city for dead. But he rose up and soon went with Barnabas to Derbe. From whence they returned to Lystra, Iconium and Antioch in Pisidia; confirming the souls of the believers. They now passed through Pamphylia to Perga and went down to Attalia.

There they sailed to Seleucia and reached Antioch in Syria; from whence they had started. Here they told their adventures to the Church, and remained teaching of Jesus.

REVIEW.

Were any believers in Jesus found in Antioch of Syria?
Who was sent to them to teach Jesus to them more perfectly?
For whom did Barnabas go to Tarsus? Why?
By what name was Paul before known?
Do you remember anything of his former life?
Did Paul come to Antioch?
How long were these teachers busy in Antioch?
Tell what now befell Jerusalem.
How did the people at Antioch aid those at Jerusalem?
What name was first given to the disciples of Jesus in Antioch?
Did Barnabas and Paul tarry long in Jerusalem?
Upon what great work did they start?
Whom did they take with them? Acts 12: 12.
Into what lands did they travel?
At Paphos what happened to Elymas? And why?
How did the Jews and Gentiles receive the truth at Antioch in Pisidia?
What glorious promise comes to those who call upon Jesus in faith?
What act of mercy was done at Lystra?
Seeing this wonder, what did the people imagine?
How were they about to honor the apostles?
Did the apostles explain who they were?
How was poor Paul afterwards treated by the Jews? II. Cor. 11: 25.
Did the apostles now return?
Can you describe their route?
On arriving at Antioch of Syria what did they do?
Is God with us in times of danger as well as when we are in safety?

Notes. [It is a good plan to let the scholar follow the missionaries if possible and trace their route from point to point upon the map, viz: Antioch in Syria, Jerusalem, Antioch, Seleucia, Cyprus, Salamis, Paphos, Pamphylia, Perga, Pisidia, Antioch in Pisidia, Iconium, Derbe, Lystra, Derbe, Lystra, Iconium, Antioch in Pisidia, Perga, Attalia, Seleucia, Antioch in Syria.] SALVATION, being made safe from sin and death. CHRISTIANS, believers in and followers of Christ. FAMINE, a time of scarcity in the whole land. JOURNEY, a travel day by day. MAGICIAN, a performer of tricks who claims supernatural power. GODS, false deities which the heathen ignorantly worshiped. JUPITER, the King of all false gods. MERCURY, that heathen deity who bore messages. FURIOUS, raging. UPROAR, excitement, riot. CONFIRMING, making strong and sure. ADVENTURES, those events one meets in life, acts, exploits and experiences.

Lesson 46.—The Sixteenth Sunday after Trinity.

THE COUNCIL AT JERUSALEM AND THE EPISTLES.

COMMIT THE NAMES OF THE NEW TESTAMENT BOOKS. READ ACTS 15: 1—35.

THE STORY.

Certain Jewish Christians disputed with Paul and Barnabas while at Antioch, saying: "It is needful to circumcise the Gentile Christians and compel them to keep the Jewish Law."

In order to decide this matter, **Paul and Barnabas** went to Jerusalem to consult the apostles.

Then the apostles and Elders held a Council at Jerusalem. Peter showed that God made no distinction between the circumcised Jews and uncircumcised Gentiles; and told of his vision at Joppa. All true believers in Jesus shall be saved.

Barnabas and Paul told of their great success, and the miracles they had wrought among the Gentiles. Then James spoke, saying that the law of the Lord was fulfilled by active faith; and did not require the keeping by the Gentiles of the old Jewish law of mere outward works. It was enough if the true followers of Jesus abstained from meat sacrificed to idols; and from the drinking of blood, as heathens did; from eating animals strangled to death and from fornication, a most horrible and shameful sin which many a heathen committed. This advice was sent, by the Council, in a letter to the Christians at Antioch, carried by Barnabas and Paul, who were accompanied by Judas and Silas.

On arriving at Antioch, Paul and Barnabas delivered the letter from the Council in Jerusalem; and encouraged and confirmed the believers of Antioch in their faith and zeal.

Later in life the apostles wrote many letters, called "Epistles", to the Churches and Christians in various lands and cities. Paul, it is thought, wrote 14; viz: to Thessalonica twice, to Galatia, to Corinth twice, to Rome, to Philippi, to Colosse, to Ephesus, to his friends Philemon, Timothy twice, Titus; and to the Hebrews, or Jews.

The Church in all places received a general letter from the apostle James, two from Peter, three from John and one from Jude. These Epistles are all found in the New Testament in their proper order. Each holy page contains some precious instruction needed in the apostles' time and most profitable now

REVIEW.

Tell what dispute arose at Antioch.
How did some Jewish Christians think and speak?
How did Paul and Barnabas act in this matter?
To whom did they go?
And what did the apostles and elders do?
At the Council what did Peter tell and declare?
What four duties only were enjoined upon all Christians? Lev. 17:14. 1st Com. 6th Com.
How was this advice sent?
Did any come with Paul and Barnabas to Antioch?
On arriving what did the travelers Barnabas and Paul do?
In the later days, what were sent by the apostles to Churches and Christians?
How many letters is Paul supposed to have written?
Can you name them?
How many were from James' hand?
How many did Peter send? John? Jude?
In what great Book are all these Epistles found?
Do these Epistles contain instruction that is useful to us?

Notes. COUNCIL, the meeting of the teachers and representatives of the Church to decide questions of faith and practice. EPISTLES, letters. NEW TESTAMENT, that wonderful Book which "testifies" of Jesus Christ, called "New" to distinguish it from the former half of the Bible, the "Old Testament", which promised Christ to the world. JEWISH CHRISTIANS, the believers in Christ who had been Jews. DISPUTED, did not think alike, nor agree. NEEDFUL, necessary, indispensable. GENTILE CHRISTIANS, believers in Christ who had been Gentiles, or heathen. DECIDE, to form and give an opinion. CONSULT, to find each other's opinion. ELDERS OF THE CHURCH, those old and responsible men who were officers and teachers in the congregation. From their duty of supervision they were often called "Bishops" [i. e. overseers.] DISTINCTION, separation, division. SUCCESS, good hopes and plans fulfilled. ABSTAIN, to keep away from. MEATS, the meat offered by heathen to idols was often sold afterward by the priests in the markets. BLOOD, the ancients believed the spirit, or life to be in the blood [Gen. 9: 4]. Hence the Jews were forbidden by the Lord to use it. The sacrifice of blood meant "life for life". STRANGLED, killed but not drained of blood. Lev. 17 13. FORNICATION, the crime of living as man and wife without marriage. This vile practice was strictly prohibited by the apostles. HORRIBLE, causing fear. ENCOURAGED, made more brave. THESSALO-NI-CA, a famous city on the shore of Macedonia. GA-LA-TIA, a country in the centre of Asia Minor. COR-INTH, one of the largest cities of Greece. ROME, the great city of Italy. The home of Cæsar the Emperor. PHILIPPI, a city of Macedonia. PHI-LE-MON, a man of Colosse, master of Onesimus. CO-LOS-SE, a city of Phrygia in Asia Minor. EPH-ESUS, a grand city, the capital of Asia Minor. TIMOTHY, TITUS, disciples of Paul. JUDE, the supposed relative of our Lord. Matt. 13: 55.

Lesson 47.—The Seventeenth Sunday after Trinity.

THE MISSIONARIES PAUL, SILAS AND TIMOTHY.

COMMIT ACTS 16: 29, 30, 31. READ ACTS 15: 36—41. 16. 17. 18: 1—22.

THE STORY.

Paul and Barnabas now began to undertake another missionary journey; but Paul could not agree about taking Mark with them, who before had forsaken them and returned to Jerusalem. So Barnabas, taking Mark as his helper, sailed away to Cyprus. Paul chose Silas and departed through Syria and Cilicia preaching and teaching.

Passing through Derbe, Paul and Silas came to Lystra, where they found Timothy, a pious young man, well taught in the Scriptures by his faithful mother and grandmother. They invited him to journey with them and he did so. Churches grew in number and the missionaries went onward through Phrygia, Galatia, Mysia and came to Troas.

Here Paul saw, in a vision, a man of Macedonia, who said: "Come over into Macedonia and help us." They departed into Macedonia, came to Samothracia, Neapolis and Philippi. Here Lydia, a seller of purple cloth, became a Christian; and, with her household, was baptized. Paul and Silas here drove out (by power from the Lord) the evil "spirit of divination", by which a certain maid had long been possessed. For this kindness they were pursued by her angry masters, (who had gained much money by her pretended fortune-telling) and were caught and led to the rulers of the city followed by an excited mob.

The rulers then commanded that they be beaten, sent to prison and their feet placed in the stocks. At midnight, while poor Paul and Silas prayed and sang praises to God, suddenly there was a great earthquake and the foundations of the prison were shaken, the doors flew open and every prisoner's chains were loosened. The jailer awoke, and, seeing the open doors, was about to kill himself for fear. But Paul and Silas cried: "Do thyself no harm for we are all here." The jailer with a

Paul and Lydia.

light came to the prisoners, and, finding all safe, believed in the God of Paul and Silas. He and all his family were baptized. Next day the officers of the city, finding that they had beaten a Roman citizen without a trial, came and begged the apostles to depart. So, after they had bidden the believers in Lydia's house farewell, they went to Amphipolis and Apollonia; came to

Thessalonica, where they found a synagogue, and remained among the Jews there for a short time. But the Jews drove them away; so the apostles went on to Berea. Here the noble people daily searched the Scriptures as to whether Paul's teachings were true. But the Jews of Thessalonica came and stirred up the people. Paul now went on alone to Athens. In that great city, on Mars' Hill, he spoke to all of Jesus our Saviour, the God unknown to the people, but "in Whom all live and move and have their being." Paul again met Silas and Timothy at Corinth. Every man in those days had a trade. Paul was a tentmaker, and labored at Corinth with Aquila and his wife Priscilla (tent-makers), whom, with many, he taught to believe in Jesus.

After a year and six months Paul returned to Ephesus and sailed to Cæsarea, went to Jerusalem and then came once more to Antioch.

REVIEW.

For what did Paul and Barnabas now **prepare**?
On whose account did they separate?
To what land did Barnabas and Mark go?
Whom did Paul choose?
Into what countries did they go?
At Lystra whom did they find?
Describe Timothy, II. Timothy 1: 5. 3: 15—17.
Did Timothy follow Paul and Silas?
Did the Church grow?
At Troas what vision had Paul?
Did he listen to the cry?
At Philippi who became a Christian?
Did Paul perform a miracle here?
Did this cause any trouble?
How did the apostles bear their punishment?
How did the Lord show that He was still with them?
Had this a good effect upon the jailer?
Who beside the jailer were baptized?
Who came to ask the apostles to depart?   Why?
To what places did they go?
How did the Jews at Thessalonica receive them?
What did the noble Bereans do?   John 5: 39.
To what great city did Paul now go?
What did he do in Athens?
In Whom do we all live?   John 5: 40.
By Whom are we all saved?

In what city did Paul, Silas, and Timothy meet again?
What was Paul's trade?
With whom did he labor? How long?
Describe his return to Jerusalem and Antioch.

Notes. Let the pupil find on the map and trace the route of the Missionaries thus: Antioch, Cyprus, Syria, Cilicia, Derbe, Lystra, Phrygia, Galatia, Mysia, Troas, Macedonia, Samothracia, Neapolis, Philippi, Amphipolis, Apollonia, Thessalonica, Berea, Athens, Corinth, Ephesus, Cæsarea, Jerusalem, Antioch. PURPLE, the royal color among the ancients, the dye of which was obtained from a shell fish. SPIRIT OF DIVINATION, a false spirit of saying pretended wise things, or seeming to tell the future POSSESSED, attached to, afflicted with. STOCKS, places of punishment into which wrists or ancles were locked. SEARCHED, hunted for with care and attention. MARS' HILL, a hill in the midst of the city of Athens, on which public meetings were held. BEING existence, or life. TENT-MAKER, a common trade in ancient days.

Lesson 48.—The Eighteenth Sunday after Trinity.

PAUL'S THIRD MISSIONARY JOURNEY.

COMMIT I. CORINTHIANS 15: 10, 11. READ ACTS 18: 23 TO 21: 17.

THE STORY.

The apostle Paul soon started upon a third journey. Leaving Antioch he passed through Galatia and Phrygia, and reached Ephesus. Here Paul taught and healed the people for two years; till the Name of Jesus was great in Ephesus. Now, in that city stood a grand temple of the idol Diana; and Demetrius, a silversmith, a heathen idolmaker, jealous lest his trade should be ruined by all men turning to Jesus of Whom Paul taught, raised a frightful uproar against the Christians; the mob crying "Great is Diana of the Ephesians".

So the apostle departed into Macedonia and Achaia, and received a contribution to carry to the poor of the Church at Jerusalem.

He then returned to Philippi and Troas. Here he partook in the Lord's Supper with the disciples and restored to life young Eutychus; who, while asleep, fell from an upper window and was taken up dead.

Paul and many friends went on from Troas to Assos; then to Mitylene, Chios and Samos. Passing Trogyllium also, they met at Miletus the Elders of the Church of Ephesus. After a very affectionate meeting, Paul sailed away, having given many words of counsel and offered prayer.

PAUL'S THIRD MISSIONARY JOURNEY.

The company (for many friends were now with Paul), sailed to Coos, Rhodes, and Patara. Passing the great island of Cyprus they landed at Tyre and encouraged the disciples there. These begged Paul not to go to Jerusalem, for fear of the Jews. Not to be turned aside from duty, Paul took leave of them and

Paul leaving the Elders of Ephesus.

journeyed to Ptolemais and Cæsarea, where he abode for a time with Philip.

A prophet, Agabus, now came down from Jerusalem, and taking Paul's girdle, bound himself hand and foot, saying: "So shall the Jews at Jerusalem bind the man that owneth this girdle, and shall deliver him into the hands of the Gentiles." Paul nobly said: "I am ready not to be bound only but also to die for the Name of the Lord Jesus."

At length Paul and his fellow travelers came to Jerusalem, and were gladly met by the brethren. The next day a meeting was held by the Christians and Paul carefully told all that the Lord had done in the journey of His apostle. He presented also the gifts sent from Macedonia for the poor.

REVIEW.

Did Paul now cease from his labor for the Lord?
How did he reach Ephesus?
Did he perform any miracles there?
Had this a good effect upon the people?
Tell what great building stood in Ephesus.
On what account was an uproar raised in that city?
By whom was it begun?
What did the people shout?
To what lands did Paul depart?
Did he receive anything in Macedonia? II. Cor. 8: 1—15.
Relate the wonderful act of Paul at Troas.
Did Paul return to Ephesus?
But where did he meet the Elders of the Ephesian Church?
Can you describe their meeting with Paul?
Did Paul now travel alone?
Did he go from Miletus by land or sea?
Past what great island did they sail?
At what city did they land?
How did Paul bless the Church at Tyre?
Did the men of Tyre beg Paul not to go to Jerusalem? Why?
But would Paul neglect his duty through fear? Luke 9: 62.
At whose house in Cæsarea did Paul tarry? Acts 8: 40. 21: 8—10.
Describe the Prophecy given to Paul here.
By whom was it given?
Have you heard of any other who was thus delivered to the Gentiles? Mark 10: 33. Acts 2: 23.
How did Paul nobly answer?
For what was Paul ready? II. Tim. 4: 6.
Did Paul's company at last reach Jerusalem?
How were they met?
On the next day what took place?
What had Paul to present?

Notes. The Route of Paul's third journey, as given, is: — from Antioch in Syria, through the lands of Galatia and Phrygia, to the city of Ephesus. Thence to Macedonia and Achaia [Greece], returning to Philippi, Troas, Assos, Mitylene, the islands Coos, Rhodes, the city Patara, the island Cyprus, the cities Tyre, Ptolemais, Cæsarea, Jerusalem. Trace if possible this course on the map. TARRIED, remained. DIANA, an idol goddess of the heathen at Ephesus. Her ebony figure was supposed to have fallen from heaven. Images of it were made by silversmiths and carried to all parts of Asia Minor, to be worshiped. SILVERSMITH, one whose trade is the making of silver shrines; the silversmith at Ephesus, a man whose main trade was the making of images of Diana and like work. CONTRIBUTION, one part of a gift made up by many persons. AFFECTIONATE, loving. COUNSEL, advice. ABODE, found a resting place, or home. READY, prepared and willing.

Lesson 49.—The Nineteenth Sunday after Trinity.
PAUL A PRISONER.
COMMIT ACTS 23: 11.   READ ACTS 21: 17 TO 28: 31.   II. CORINTHIANS 11: 21 TO 12: 10.

THE STORY.

When Paul had finished the telling of his history to the Church at Jerusalem he reverently went into the Temple, to fulfill a vow he had made. The Jews saw Paul walking in the city with his Greek friend Trophimus, and, because they *supposed* that he had brought Trophimus into the Jewish Temple, which it was not lawful for Gentiles to enter; they took Paul prisoner; and beat him, amid great excitement and disorder. The captain of the guard hurried from the Castle with soldiers, chained Paul and then gave him liberty to speak. When he spoke of his love for the poor Gentiles and his work as a missionary among them, the mob who hated Gentiles became angry and would have killed Paul if the Captain would not have taken him into the Castle. The next day Paul was tried by the Council of the Jews. The Lord appeared to Paul, encouraging him to be steadfast. So greatly did the Jews hate Paul, that some even bound themselves by an oath not to eat or drink till they had killed Paul. This plot was found out, and Lysias sent Paul away, guarded, to Felix the Roman Governor of Judea at Cæsarea. As Paul before Felix reasoned of righteousness, temperance and judgment to come, he trembled, for he was a great sinner. Just to please the Jews, Felix kept Paul a prisoner; and two years later gave him over to the new Governor Festus. Festus heard Paul plead for liberty, and when Agrippa, King of Chalcis, visited Festus, Paul was again tried; and spoke so nobly that Agrippa said: "Almost thou persuadest me to be a Christian."

Paul, being a "Roman citizen", begged to be sent for trial to *Cæsar*, the great Emperor at Rome. He was allowed to go.

Under guards, with other prisoners, he started from Cæsarea to Sidon, sailed past Cyprus, Cilicia, Pamphylia; changed ships at Myra of Lycia, passed Cnidus and Salmone of the island Crete, and reached the Fair Havens near Lasea. They should have gone no further, as the winter was approaching, but they sailed onward; hoping to reach the harbor of Phenice.

Paul taken Prisoner.

But when near a small island, Clauda, they were suddenly caught in a furious tempest, and the little ship was driven out of its course for fourteen days of clouds and darkness. But an angel appeared to Paul, saying that though the ship would be lost all would escape to land.

After being so long tossed the vessel neared a certain island, Melita, (Malta), and was run aground and wrecked.

But by swimming, or clinging to broken pieces of the ship, all reached the shore alive.

The people of the island received the strangers kindly. Paul gathered sticks for a fire, and, in doing so, found that a viper was clinging to his arm. When the heathen people saw this, they thought that Paul must be a great criminal; for, though he had escaped the sea, the goddess of Justice would kill him by the serpent's bite. But he shook off the viper into the fire and felt no harm. Then the savage people said: "He is a god!"

The chief man of the island was Publius, whose father was sick with fever. Paul healed him and many others also. Then the people honored Paul and his friends. After three winter months the soldiers departed with their prisoners to Syracuse, Rhegium, **Puteoli**, **Appii Forum**, and, at last, reached Rome.

Here Paul was allowed to live in his own rented house, chained to a soldier that kept him; and was busy in preaching to Jews and Gentiles the good news of forgiveness and life to all who believe in Jesus Christ our Saviour. Here the story of Paul's life is ended by St. Luke. It is supposed that he was put to death in Rome by the cruel Emperor Nero, some years later.

REVIEW.

Should Christians rejoice to see each other?
Did Paul forget his duty to God's house?
How did the Jews suppose that Paul had done wrong?
Had the Jews malice in their hearts?
How did they act?
By whom was Paul saved?
Did Paul speak to the mob?
For what were they angry?
Before whom was he tried next day?
What did the Captain do with Paul?
Why was this necessary?
How was Paul encouraged?
To whom was Paul sent? Name the Captain.
At hearing Paul why did Felix tremble?
But why was Paul not set free?
Before whom was Paul also tried?
What did Agrippa confess?
To whom was Paul sent away?
Can you trace his journey to Crete?
Relate what terrible adventure befell the ship?

What island did they reach?
Had it not been for that island must they have been driven much farther?
Who cares for us and knows us in our greatest dangers? Ps. 130.
Tell what became of the ship.
Did Paul know this? How?
Did any of the voyagers drown?
How were they received?
Tell why different opinions were formed of Paul.
Did Paul do any good?
How long did all remain at Malta?
To what great city did they finally come?
In what way did Paul live?
In what way, do we read, that this holy, noble and useful man was engaged to the last?
How is he supposed to have died?
Should we be almost or altogether a Christian?
What is a Christian?

Notes. Trace if you can on the map, Paul's voyage as follows: Cæsarea, Sidon, Cyprus, Cilicia; Pamphylia, Myra, in Lycia; Cnidus, Crete, Salmone, Fair Havens, Phenice, Clauda, Melita [Malta], Syracuse, Rhegium, Puteoli, Appii-Forum, Rome. Vow, a solemn promise. The vow made by Paul was doubtless to abstain from wine and after shearing to wear the hair uncut for thirty days previous to offering a sacrifice in the Temple at Jerusalem. GREEK, a Gentile from Greece. EXCITEMENT, a stir, or disturbance of mind. CAPTAIN, the chief Roman soldier of the Temple guard. ANGRY, displeased. CASTLE, the military barracks and prison at the N. W. corner of the court of the Temple. It was named the Tower of Antonia. RIGHTEOUSNESS, the state of being right. TEMPERANCE, self control, moderation in all things. JUDGMENT, separation between good and evil. AGRIPPA, this king was the great grandson of Herod the great. CITIZEN, a man having rights and liberties in a city. GOD, this term is used to express a false deity.

Lesson 50.—The Twentieth Sunday after Trinity.

THE TAKING OF JERUSALEM AND THE BANISHMENT OF ST. JOHN.

COMMIT MATTHEW 24: 13. READ MATTHEW 24: 1—28. LUKE 19: 41—45. REVELATION 1: 1—11. 21: 10 TO 22: 21.

THE STORY.

Pontius Pilate, Felix, Festus, Albinus and Gessius Florus, in turn ruled the conquered Jews as Roman governors, or Procurators appointed by Caesar. Each tried by cruel ways to arouse the discontent of the people and cause an insurrection so as to conquer the weak Jews the more thoroughly. At last they succeeded; and, in the year 70, the rebellion of the Jews broke out during the Passover, when Jerusalem was crowded with people.

Disputes, famine and pestilence raged in the great city that was surrounded by the Roman army under general Titus, son of the Emperor Vespasian. Many died of starvation or disease and others were crucified by the cruel Romans who captured the city. The beautiful Temple was consumed by fire and crumbled to the ground. The soldiers triumphantly brought to Rome and displayed the Table of Shewbread, the golden Candlestick, the Book of the Law and other precious things from the Temple at Jerusalem.

The Jews fled and ever since have been scattered among the nations. In the year of our Lord 120, Hadrian the Emperor, rebuilt Jerusalem, but the Jews were forbidden to enter it under penalty of death.

After the Christian congregations of Asia Minor had lost their faithful Paul, the loving apostle John was sent to them. He dwelt in Ephesus for a long time, and it is supposed was the last of the apostles to die. The Emperor Domitian banished the aged John to the lonely island of Patmos, and it was there that the Lord granted to him glorious visions, of which he wrote in the book called "The Revelation", about the year 96. This Book, the prophecy of the New Testament, God will fulfill in all its glory in Heaven; at the end of the New Covenant and of the world; when those who have believed in Christ, and are saved by His Atonement and Pleading, are raised by His power and shall live forever with Him. The Book of the Revelation completes the Bible.

REVIEW.

Name for me the five Roman governors of Judea.
How were they appointed?
What did they seek to do?
Is it a sin to be cruel?
Did they succeed? In what year?
At what time of the year?
Name the conqueror of Jerusalem.
Did many Jews die? From what causes?
Tell what became of the Temple. See Matt. 24: 2 etc.
Did Titus carry anything to Rome?
After the war did the Jews regain Jerusalem?
How long was the city desolate?
By whom was it rebuilt?

After the city was rebuilt were the Jews allowed to return to Jerusalem?
How where those who disobeyed punished?
After Paul's capture which apostle came to Asia Minor?
Can you describe his disposition?
Do you remember anything you have learned of his previous life?
In what city did he reside?
What is supposed about his age?
Did the Emperor banish the aged John?
To what rocky island?
How did the Lord grant His favor to John?
Can you tell what kind of a book the Revelation is?
About what year was it written?
Shall it be fulfilled?
What becomes of those who love and believe in Christ? Apos. Creed Art 3. See Catech. Part II.
What place in the Holy Bible has this Book?

Notes. BANISHMENT, being driven from one's home, or country. GOVERNOR, a ruler in the name of the Emperor, the chief man of a province. [Pilate is recorded as governor A. D. 27 to 37, Felix 44 to 60, Porcius Festus 60 to 62, Albinus 62 to 66, Gessius Florus 66 to 70.] DISCONTENT, dissatisfaction. CONQUERED, completely subdued. The Jewish nation instead of being tributary and separate, by this conquest lost their nationality; being merged into the vast Roman Empire itself. INSURRECTION, the rising of a people against their rulers. REBELLION, war against the constitutional authority. PESTILENCE, a general spread of any disease. BESIEGED, encircled by an army of enemies waiting, or fighting for the surrender of a city. CONSUMED, eaten away or destroyed as by fire. CRUMBLED, became dust, or ashes. DISPLAYED, shown plainly, set forth. PATMOS, an island of rocks in the Ægean Sea, not far from Miletus and Ephesus. REVELATION, an unclosing or showing of what had not been seen, known, or understood

---

Lesson 51.—The Twenty-first Sunday after Trinity.

A LESSON IN REVIEW.

COMMIT I. JOHN 5: 11, 12, 13. READ JOHN 1: 1 TO 5. I. JOHN 1 REV. CH. 1 TO 5, 21, 22.

THE STORY.

The closing part of the Bible tells us of the planting of the Holy Christian Church. At Pentecost, ten days after our Saviour had ascended to heaven, the Holy Spirit came to the disciples in the appearance as of cloven flames of fire, with a sound as of a strongly rushing wind and the gift of speaking and teaching, in many languages, of Jesus.

Many heard and learned to believe in their Saviour.

The fanatical Jews followed the success of the apostles with the persecution of the Church. Some were imprisoned but released by angels and continued to speak of Jesus. Others were scattered and preached the gospel of Christ everywhere. Seven Deacons were chosen to aid the apostles and elders in their work, of helping the poor. Of these, Stephen became the first martyr and Philip the first missionary among the Samaritans. In the Name of Jesus, he baptized a noble officer of Ethiopia.

A great change was wrought in Saul of Tarsus. Though a bitter persecutor of the Church he received a vision of the Lord, was baptized and lived a changed life as Paul; a strong believer and most diligent laborer for Christ.

The apostle Peter visited Lydda, Joppa, Caesarea, and at each place wonderful events took place. He then returned to Jerusalem.

Barnabas, Paul and Mark now set forth as missionaries upon a long journey through Asia Minor. Having done much good, they returned to Antioch in Syria, where the disciples were first named "Christians".

At Jerusalem a council was held. The Church decided that the poor heathen Gentiles, on becoming Christians, were not required to obey all the outward works of the old Jewish law, but to perform such duties alone as were signs of their love and trust in Jesus our Saviour.

Many letters concerning Jesus passed from the hands of the apostles to the Churches and Christians. Fourteen are ascribed to Paul, one to James, two to Peter, three to John and one to Jude.

Paul, with Silas and Timothy for companions, now undertook a second journey; Barnabas and Mark having gone to Cyprus to teach. Paul now reached the people of Athens and Corinth in Greece. After a long absence he came back to Antioch.

He undertook, later, a third journey among the Churches of Asia Minor, Macedonia and Greece. On his return many friends came with him to Jerusalem.

But the envious Jews of that city, seized him on a false charge of breaking the law, and Paul was led into the Castle of Antonia and afterward sent to Caesarea.

A Lesson in Review.

After many appeals and a long imprisonment he was sent for trial to Caesar at Rome in Italy. During the long voyage the vessel was shipwrecked at the island Malta, but all lives were spared. At last Paul reached Rome a prisoner and lived there at least two years longer. It is supposed that the Emperor Nero put him to death in Rome.

Jerusalem was taken by Titus of Rome, the Temple was burned and the people scattered.

The last living apostle John, an exile upon rocky Patmos, saw and wrote that glorious Revelation of the Lord which closes the Bible, the Word of God to man.

REVIEW.

Of what does the last part of the Bible speak?
How was the Holy Spirit manifested at Pentecost?
By what did the Jews show their hatred?
Who helped the apostles?
What officers were appointed to aid the apostles?
Can you tell what befell Stephen?
How did Philip fare?
Describe the great change that took place in Saul.
By what name was he afterward known?
Did he labor diligently for the Lord?
To what cities did Peter go?
Tell me what miracles he wrought.
Describe Paul's first missionary journey (route, companions etc.).
In what place were the disciples first called Christians?
How did the council at Jerusalem advise the Gentiles as to Jewish duties?
Of what should all Christian works be signs?
What are Epistles?
By whom were the Epistles mentioned written?
Can you relate anything about Paul's second missionary journey?
Tell also where the third journey was made.
After Paul had come to Jerusalem for the third time, what became of him?
What sad history closes the record of Jerusalem?
Who was John?
What grand book which he wrote completes the Bible?
Tell me, what is the Bible?

Notes. PLANTING, setting a living seed or root in the earth, establishing. CLOVEN, divided. TEACHING, causing another to know. FANATICAL, furious in religion. SUCCESS, achievement, victory. RELEASED, set free. SCATTERED, separated, driven apart. AID, help. DILIGENT, earnest and active. ASIA MINOR, that populous region of Asia lying between the Black and the Mediterranean Seas. REQUIRED, compelled. ASCRIBED, declared to be the work of a certain person. APPEALS, earnest requests.

CASTLE OF ANTONIA, the chief citadel of Jerusalem named by King Herod after Mark Antony a noted Roman. TITUS, a noted general afterward Emperor A. D. 79—81. EXILE, banishment.

Lesson 52.—The Twenty-second Sunday after Trinity.

A GENERAL REVIEW.

COMMIT THE NAMES OF THE BOOKS OF THE BIBLE. READ MATTHEW 5, 6, 7. JOHN 12: 23—50.

THE STORY.

We have reached the end of the Bible's holy History. Let us think of what we have learned. In six days the world was made. Adam and Eve were in Eden. But our first parents disobeyed, fell into sin and the LORD sent them out of Eden to die. Yet God promised, graciously to them a SAVIOUR, from eternal death. Cain, the first son, killed his brother Abel.

Enoch (and the prophet Elijah also) was carried to heaven without death.

The wicked people were destroyed by a flood and all, save Noah's family, were drowned. Forgetful sinners toiled to build the Tower of Babel. Abraham, Isaac and Jacob (Israel) in covenant with God received wonderful promises of the SAVIOUR. Joseph and his eleven brothers became the founders of the tribes of the Jewish nation, whom Moses and Aaron delivered from slavery. The Lord now gave His Law, (the Ten Commandments) and His Name was praised in the Tabernacle.

Moses led the Israelites forty years. Then Joshua led them into the "Promised Land", dividing it among them. Fifteen Judges ruled, Ruth gleaned, and Samuel the High Priest anointed, in turn, Saul and David as Kings over Israel (the Jews).

Then wise Solomon sat as King and erected the grand Temple. Under King Rehoboam the nation was divided into the Kingdom of Israel and the Kingdom of Judah.

By the taking of the Kingdom of Israel, (whose Kings were all idolaters) to Assyria, the "Ten Tribes" were scattered and lost.

The two Tribes (Judah and Benjamin), after seventy years of captivity in Babylon, returned to Jerusalem. Mordecai and Esther at Babylon saved the Jews from destruction. The Temple was rebuilt at Jerusalem after the Jews' return and many promises of the coming Messiah were given by the prophets. Holy Types also reminded of Him.

After John the Baptist had come to teach all men to repent and to point all men to the Saviour, in due time JESUS began to teach. He died in punishment for the sins of the whole world, so as to save such as depend upon Him in faith.

We have learned of His *Birth*, His *Baptism* and *Temptation*, of His *Parables* and *Miracles*, of His *Apostles* and the *Founding of His Church, or Kingdom*; of His glorious *Transfiguration*, of His *Sufferings*, His *Cross*, His *Death*, His *Burial*, His *Resurrection* and His glorious *Ascension* to Heaven.

By the *Coming of the Holy Spirit* the Apostles were made strong to endure patiently the persecution that befell them, earnestly to teach and labor for Christ, and to be steadfast as Bishops (Elders), Deacons and brethren.

We have read of the noble lives of John, Peter, Stephen, Philip and Barnabas. Saul becoming the faithful Paul and an "Apostle to the Gentiles" made three great Missionary journeys in heathen lands.

The first general Council of the Church was held at Jerusalem. Many letters were sent to the Churches by the apostles.

Paul became a prisoner and was sent to Rome.

Jerusalem was taken by the Romans and destroyed.

The aged apostle John wrote the Book of the glorious Revelation of Heaven which he had received from God: thus completing the Book of God; the truth concerning Jesus Christ.

REVIEW.

In how many days were all things made?
A great wrong was done by Adam and Eve, what was it?
Tell me what was Cain's great sin?
Two men did not die: can you give their names?
How were all the wicked ones destroyed?
Who were saved?
For what was the Tower of Babel begun?
Why was it not finished?
For what were Abraham, Isaac and Jacob remarkable?
Had Jacob another name?
About Whom were promises given from God?
How did Joseph establish the Jewish nation?
By whom was it delivered from slavery?

Did the LORD show His constant care of Israel? Deut. 32: 7—12. Ps. 46: 7.

How long did Moses lead Israel?

By whom was he succeeded?

How many Judges in turn followed?

Tell what you know of Samuel. Of Ruth. Of Saul. Of David.

Why had a Saviour been promised to the world even in the garden of Eden? Gen. 3: 15. Is. 2: 2. 9: 6, 7. Matthew 1: 21.

How did Solomon show his wisdom?

Tell what he built.

How and why was the Kingdom of the Jews divided?

What became of the ten Tribes?

Did Judah return after captivity? Ezra 1: 1—4.

Tell what Esther did.

Had the later Jews more promises of Christ?

By whom was the Saviour announced and baptized?

What can you tell me about His Birth? His Baptism? His Temptation? His Transfiguration? His Sufferings and Death? His Resurrection? His Ascension?

Can you tell the meaning of the word Parable? Of Miracle? Of Apostle? Of Disciple?

Why did Jesus come to the world? John 3: 16.

Are all who believe united with Him? Acts 19: 4, 5. II. Cor. 5: 17. Heb. 7: 25.

How did the apostles receive the gift of His Spirit?

Tell what they then were able to do.

Mention some of the apostles and Christians of those days.

How many journeys did Paul make?

What great meeting was held at Jerusalem?

What are Epistles?

How did Paul's labor cease?

Can you name the 39 Old Testament and 27 New Testament Books?

By whom was Jerusalem taken and destroyed?

A Book of prophecy completes the New Testament, what is it?

By whom was it written?

Notes. HISTORY, the story of human events. FORGETFUL, not thoughtful, not remembering. HEAVEN, the city of the holy and the good, into which the repentant sinner saved from eternal death is brought by union with his Saviour Jesus Christ, in true faith. The place of the Throne and Presence of the Triune God.

A CONCISE CHRONOLOGY

OF

PRINCIPAL BIBLE EVENTS.

BEFORE CHRIST.

4004	Adam	1015	Solomon the third King
3382	Enoch born	975	The Kingdom divided
2948	Noah born	975	Rehoboam, King of Judah
2348	The Flood began	975	Jeroboam, King of Israel
2245	The Tower of Babel	958	Abijah Judah
1996	Abram born	955	Asa "
1896	Isaac born	955	Nadab, King of Israel
1836	Esau and Jacob born	953	Baasha, King of Israel
1706	Jacob goes to Egypt	929	Elah "
1600	Job (?)	927	Zimri 7 days "
1571	Moses born	927	Omri "
1491	The Exodus begins	918	Ahab "
1451	Canaan is entered	914	Jehoshaphat Judah
1451	Joshua begins to rule	896	Ahaziah, Israel
1426	15 Elders rule	896	Jehoram } "
1409	Othniel judges Israel	889	Jehoram } Judah
1369	Ehud " "	885	Ahaziah "
1356	Shamgar " "	884	Jehu, Israel
1338	Deborah and Barak judge Israel	884	Queen Athalia, Judah
		878	Joash, "
1291	Gideon judges Israel	857	Jehoahaz, King of Israel
1251	Abimelech " "	840	Joash " "
1251	Tola " "	839	Amaziah, Judah
1228	Jair " "	825	Jeroboam II., Israel
1206	Jephtha " "	810	Uzziah, Judah
1200	Ibzan " "	784	Anarchy in Israel
1193	Elon " "	773	Zacharias "
1183	Abdon " "	773	Shallum "
1175	Samson " "	773	Menahem "
1155	Eli, High Priest	763	Pekahiah "
1115	Samuel " "	761	Pekah "
1095	Saul the first King	758	Jotham, King of Judah
1055	David the second King	742	Ahaz, King of Judah
		739	Anarchy in Israel

A Chronology of Bible Events.

730	Hoshea in Israel
726	Hezekiah in Judah
721	The Assyrian Captivity
698	Manasseh Judah
643	Amon "
641	Josiah "
609	Jehoahaz "
609	Jehoiakim "
599	Jehoiachin "
599	Zedekiah "
588	Captivity in Babylon
536	Zerubbabel returns
516	Second Temple dedicated
468	Ezra returns
455	Nehemiah returns
330	Alexander the Great rules Jerusalem
320	Egypt takes Jerusalem
175	Syria takes Jerusalem
160	Temple restored by Judas Maccabeus
63	Rome takes Jerusalem
49	Rome makes Herod King of Judea
28	Augustus Emperor of Rome Christ is Born

AFTER CHRIST.

3	Archelaus, King of Judea. Joseph takes Mary and Jesus the Christ to Nazareth in Galilee
8	Tiberius, Emperor at Rome. Jesus in the Temple
26	Pilate procurator of Judea
27	John the Baptist appears. Jesus is baptized
33	JESUS is crucified, rises from the dead and ascends to heaven. The HOLY GHOST descends on the disciples
34	Seven Deacons, Stephen the martyr
35	The Conversion of Saul
37	Caligula Emperor of Rome
41	Claudius Emperor of Rome
45	Paul and Barnabas travel
53	Paul and Silas travel
54	Nero Emperor of Rome
56	Paul's third journey
60	Paul a prisoner
63	Paul in Rome
64	Persecution of Christians
68	Nero slays himself
68—70	Galba, Otho, Vitellius Emperors
70	Vespasian Emperor. Jerusalem taken by Titus of Rome: city and Temple destroyed
79	Titus Emperor of Rome
81	Domitian Emperor of Rome
95	Second Persecution of the Christians
96	John writes the Book of the Revelation
96	Nerva Emperor of Rome

INDEX TO THE NOTES.

A.

Abode	48
Abstain	46
Accept	44
Accused	10
Achai'a	48
Acknowledged	18
Action	33
A. D	38
Adopted	7
Adultery	10
Ad'vent	1
Adventures	45
Advice	35
Affectionate	48
Afflict	11
Afflictions	19
Agrip'pa	49
Aid	51
Aided	13
"All hail"	36
Allowed	22
Al'tar	4
Amazed	39
Amphi'polis	47
Anarchy	23
Angels	8, 17
Angry	46
Announce	28
Anointed	19
An'tioch in Pisid'ia	45
An'tioch in Sy'ria	45, 46, 47, 48
Apollo'nia	47
Apos'tles	32
Appeals	51
Appearance	34
Appeared	29
Ap'pii Fo'rum	49
Appointed	37
Ark	4
Arrogant	31
Ascen'sion	37
Ascribed	51
A'sia Mi'nor	51
Assisted	15
As'sos	48
Assyr'ia	23
Astray	20
Ath'ens	47
Atone'ment	15
At tali'a	45
Attendant	16
Au gus'tus	30
Authority	39
Awaited	44
A zo'tus	42

B.

Bab'y lon	23
Bade	13
Banishment	50
Baptism	31
Baptize'	37
Beasts	44
Beautiful	27
Begged	36
Being	47
Believing	27
Belonged	30
Beloved	31
Benevolent	44
Be re'a	47
Besieged	50
Beth'any	37
Beth'le hem of Judea	30
Betray	35
Birthright	8
Bish'ops, see Elders	46
Bitterly	42
Blessed	11
Blessing	8
Blood	35, 46
Blood and Water	35
Body	35
Boldly	39
Bond	5
Bondage	23
Booths	34
Brave	20
Brazen	15, 27
Bread	35
Breastplate	15
Bribed	25
Bronze	27
Burial	36

C.

Cæsare'a	42, 47, 48, 49
Calming	33
Cal'va ry	35
Ca'naan	14
Ca'naan ites	7
Can da'ce	42
Caper'naum	33
Captain	49
Captive	6
Captivity	26
Cast	13
Castle	49
Castle of Antonio	51
Caused	16
Ceiled	27
Censers	27
Centurion	44
Change	43
Charge	11
Chariot	28
Cherubim	27
Chi'os [$K\bar{\imath}$-os]	48
Choice	20
Choked	32
CHRIST	30
Christian Gentiles	46
Christians	45
Christmas	5
Chronological	23
Church	32
Cili cie'ia	43, 46, 49
Cir'cumcised	6
Citizen	43, 49
Claim	31
Clau'da	49
Cleansed	33
Cloven	51
Cni'dus	49
Co los'se	46
Columns	17
Comfort	11
COMFORTER	37
Command	16
Compelled	8
Confess	38
Confirming	45
Confused	1

Confusion	5, 23
Conquer	17, 50
Consecra'tion	31
Consult	46
Consumed	50
Continually	15
Continued	32
Contribu'tion	48
Convinces	39
Coos	48
Cor'inth	46, 47
Corrupt	4
Council	40, 46
Counsel	48
Courage	39
Courses	27
Court'yard	15
Cov'enant	16
Coverings	15
Crea'ted	1
Crete	49
Crime	10
Cross	35
Crowned	22
Crucify	35
Cruel	23
Crumbled	50
Crushed	32
Cup	35
Curse	11
Cy'prus	45, 46, 48, 49

D.

Damas'cus	43
Deacons	41, 42
Deception	7, 42
Decide	46
Dedicating	22
Defend	13
Defending	20, 23
Delivered	25
Der'be	46
Descendants	3
Des'ert	42
Despised	25
Destroy	4
Destruction	25
Determined	4
Devil	31
Dian'a	48

163

Index to the Notes.

Diligent	51	Feast	25
Disappearing	37	Feats	17
Disciples	29	Fled	13
Discontent	50	Forbidden	2
Disgrace	10	Forced	38
Disobedient	2	Foreign	38
Displayed	50	Forerunner	38
Disputed	46	Foretold	21
Distinction	46	Forgetful	52
Distinguished	41	Forgiven	8, 35
Distribution	41	Forgiveness	15
Divination	47	Form	31
Doctors	38	Fornication	46
Drought	28	Forsaken	10
Dream	8, 30	Forsook	20
Dwelt	9	Foster-father	30
		Founder	6
		Frankincense	30
E.		Frightened	36
		Fulfilled	31
Earthquake	35	Furious	45
Eas'ter	14, 22	Furniture	26
Egyptian	22		
Elders	24	**G.**	
Elders of the Church	46	Ga la' ti a	46, 47, 48
Embroidered	15	Ga' li lee	30
Em' maus	37	Gallows	25
Emperor	29	Game	8
Employed	13	Gardener	36
Empty	36	Garment	33
Enclosed	15	Gath'	21
Enclosure	27	Gathered	32
Encouraged	46	Ga' za	42
Enemies	17	Gazing	37
Envied	20	Generation	3
Eph'esus	46, 47, 48	Ge'n tiles	44, 46
E piph'a ny	7	Giant	20
Epistles	46	Gifts	30
Escaped	43	Girdle	15
Eternal	5	Glances	37
E thi o' pi a	42	Glorious	29
Eu' nuch	42	Glory	34
Event	25, 34	Gods	45, 49
Everlasting	32	God-like	3
Evil spirits	32	Gold	30
Exalted	25	Governor	50
Example	31	Gradually	22
Exchanged	35	Grateful	25
Excitement	49	Great	11
Exile	51	Gre'cian	41
Explain	10	Greek	49
		Grief	11
F.		Guest	25
		Guide	13
Fair Ha' vens	49		
Faith	3	**H.**	
Faithful	4		
Fall	2	Handsome	20
False	28	Happen	28
Family portion	10	Harp	21
Famine	45	Harvest	18
Fanatical	51	Hastening	36
Favorite	7		

Hated	7	Judges	17
Healed	43	Judgment	11, 49
Heathen	22	Judgment Day	39
Heaven	52	Jupiter	45
Heavenly	32	Justified	11
Hebrews	13		
Hero	17	**K.**	
Her' od	35, 38		
High Priest	13, 35	King	20
Hinder	26	Kingdoms	31
History	52	King of the Jews	35
Holy	19	Kins man	18
HOLY GHOST	36		
(See 19 and 31.)		**L.**	
Holy Land	33		
Holy Place	15	Lamented	19
Holy Supper	38	Language	5
Honest	41	Later	23
Honor	22	Lavers	27
Honored	10, 20	Laws	33
Horrible	46	Law-giver	34
Hour of Prayer	29	Laying on of hands	41
Housetop	44	Leader	16
Humble	18	Learners	32
Humility	35	Lent	16
Hymn	35	Lepers	23
		Lie	2
I.		Locusts	29
		Lodged	30
Idol	14	LORD	32
Idolater	23	Lot	24
Impatience	11	Loved	37
Impatient	20	Lyc' i a	49
Impostor	31	Lying	9
Incarnation	30	Lys'tra	46
Incense	15		
Industrious	18	**M.**	
Inn	30		
Innocent	25	Ma ce do' ni a	47, 48
Insane	21	Mag' da la	36
Inspiration	28	Ma' gi	38
Inspired	39	Magic'i an	44
Institution	32	Magnificent	27
Instruction	32	Mal' ta	49
Insurrection	50	Manger	30
In vain	33	Manifestation	34
Ish' ma el ites	9	Manna	14
Ital' ian Band	44	Manner	29
		Mantle	18, 28
J.		Mars' Hill	47
		Martyr	41
Jealous	2	Materials	27
Jealousy	8	Meats	46
JESUS	30	Melancholy	20
Je ru' sa lem	34, 46, 47	Mean	34
Jewish Christians	46	Me' li ta	49
Jews	26	Men of Galilee	37
John	29	Merciful	15
Jop' pa	44	Mer' cu ry	45
Journey	45	Messenger	33
Joy	25	MES SI' AH	38
Jude	46	Mess of Pottage	8
Ju de' a	37	Mid' i an ites	17

Index to the Notes. 165

Mi' le tus............ 48	Persecuted............ 20	Ready.................... 48	Saturday................ 36
Minister 31	Persuaded......... 17	Reared 25	Saved 14
Miracles............... 13	Pestilence............. 50	Reasoned 36	Saviour 26
Misery 11	Pharisee 43	Rebelled 23	Saving 38
Missionary........... 43	Phe ni'ce............... 49	Rebellion 60	Scarlet.................... 35
Mistrusting........... 29	Phi le'mon........... 46	Rebuilt 23	Scattered............... 51
Mitre..................... 15	Phi lip'pi...46, 47, 48	Rebuked 19	Scourge................. 35
Mit'y lene............ 48	Phi list'ines......... 17	Received 24	Seal......................... 35
Mocked 28	Phryg'i a..46, 47, 48	Records................ 25	Searched............... 47
Modest.................. 18	Pierced 35	Recovered 29	Second Coming.... 3
Mount of Olives... 35	Piety 11	Redeemer............. 37	Secretly................. 36
Multitudes............ 33	Pillaged 27	Reduced 17	Sedition 14
Murmured............ 16	Pillars 15	Referred 28	Seer........................ 28
My'ra.................... 49	Pinnacle................ 31	Refuge 16	Seized.................... 9
Myrrh................... 30	**Pious**	Reigned 3	Selected................ 41
Mys'i a................. 47	Pi sid'i a.............. 45	Rejected 19, 40	Se leu'ci a............. 45
	Plagues................. 13	Rejoiced............... 36	Selfdenying........... 18
N.	Plain 5	Released 51	Separate................ 5
Nature................... 33	Planting 51	Religion 11	Septuagesima....... 13
Nazareth of Gali-	Pleaded 25	Remained 31	Sepulchre.............. 35
lee..................... 30	Pleased 31	Remembrance..... 35	Served 8, 27
Neapolis 47	Pleasing 3	Remission 35	Settled.................... 26
Needful................. 46	Plot 25	Remorse................ 43	Sexagesima 14
Neglected............. 41	Plundered 26	Renewed 22	Shame.................... 40
New Testament 35, 46	Pontius Pilate...... 35	Rent....................... 35	Sheaves................. 9
Noble.................... 9	Possessed............ 48	Repaired 23	Shekinah............... 15
	Porch..................... 27	Repented 21	Shepherd............... 21
O.	Power.................... 39	Required 51	Shew-bread 27
	Power of the Keys 39	Rescued 6	Shield.................... 21
Obedient............... 6	Prayed 22	Rested 1	Si'don 49
Occurred............... 25	Preaching............. 37	Restored 27	Sign........................ 34
Offended 40	Precious................ 10	Resurrection 16	Silent..................... 43
Opposed................ 22	Preferred 22	Returned 23	Silver-Smith 48
Oracle.................... 27	Preparation........... 31	Revelation 50	Sin.......................... 2
Ordered................. 26	Prepare.................. 29	Revolt.................... 23	Sinner.................... 21
Orphan.................. 25	Presence............... 34	Rhe'gi um............ 49	Skill........................ 30
Overtaken............. 36	Presumption 11	Rhodes.................. 48	Slain 7
Oxen, etc.............. 35	Pretended............. 21	Rib 1	Slave...................... 9
	Pretending............ 10	Riches................... 22	Slay 11
P.	Prevented............. 5	Right'eousness..... 49	Sling....................... 21
	Priest..................... 20	Risen...................... 34	Solemn.................. 15
Pairs...................... 4	Princes.................. 38	Robe................. 15, 35	Sol'o mon............. 22
Palace.................... 13	Privilege................ 43	Ro'man................. 43	Son of God........... 30
Palm...................... 21	Promised 6	Rome 46, 49	Sorcerer................. 42
Palsied.................. 44	Prophet................. 19	Rousing................. 34	Sorrow................... 2
Pam ph'y li a.. 45, 49	Prosperity 11	Ruled..................... 18	Soul........................ 1
Panic..................... 17	Proud 2	Rulers of the Syn-	Spear...................... 21
Paphos.................. 45	Prove..................... 32	agogue............. 33	Special................... 32
Parable.................. 32	Psalms.................. 21		Speechless............. 29
Parents.................. 33	Ptol e ma' is.......... 48	**S.**	Spices.................... 36
Parted.................... 28	Punished.............. 2		Spirit..................... 29
Partition............... 44	Purifying 15	Sabbath................. 1	Spirit of God.... 31
Passion................. 35	Purple................... 47	Sacrifice................ 2	Splendid 34
Pass'o ver............. 14	Pu te'o li................ 49	Safety.................... 38	Sport...................... 17
Pat'a ra................. 48		Sake....................... 43	Spy......................... 16
Pat'mos................. 50	**Q.**	Sal'a mis............... 45	Stable..................... 30
Peace..................... 22		Sal mo' ne............ 49	Starving................. 10
Penitently............. 11	Queen.................... 38	Salvation............... 45	Steadfast................ 37
Pentecost.............. 39	Quick..................... 38	Sa ma'ri a.............. 37	Steward................. 7
Perfect................... 33	Quinquagesima.... 15	Sa mar' it ans........ 26	Stocks.................... 47
Performed............. 27		Sa'mos.................. 48	Strangers.............. 26
Per'ga.................... 45	**R.**	Sam o thra'ci a..... 47	Strangled.............. 46
Perish.................... 44	Rage...................... 20	San he'drim......... 35	Strengthen............ 33
Permitted............. 2	Rash...................... 17	Sa'tan.................... 2	Strewed................. 65

INDEX TO THE NOTES.

Subject	23	Tem'ple	27	Trusted	42	**W.**	
Sublime	22	Temptation	31	Try	6		
Success	46, 51	Tempter	31	Type	6	Warn	19
Successor	28	Tent-maker	47	Tyre	48	Washing the feet	35
Sufferings	35	Terror	20			Watchers	36
Suggested	41	Thessa lo ni'ca	46, 47	**U.**		Wealth	11
Sunday	36	Thieves	35			Welcomed	20
Supper of Life	35	Threatened	38	Understand	32	Whit-sunday	39
Supply	41	Throne	22	Unjustly	43	Wicked	4
Supposed	9	Tim'o thy	46	Upheld	16	Wilderness	7
Swathed	30	Tired	32	Uproar	45	Willful	5
Syn'a gogues	43	Titus (disciple)	46	Urged	18	Willingness	7
Syr'a cuse	49	Titus (emperor)	51			Wisdom	22
Syr'i a	47	Token	4	**V.**		Witch	20
		Traitor	35			Witnesses	37
T.		Trance	44			Wonder	22
		Transfiguration	34	Vain	25	Wonderful	28
Tab'er na cle	15	Transfigured	14	Valor	20	Worldlings	4
Tablets	13	Trembled	36	Vanished	36	Worship	14
Tarried	48	Tribe	13	Vegetation	1	Wrestled	8
Tarsus	48	TRINITY	30	Vicious	10		
Taught	9	Triumphantly	35	Virtue	18	**Z.**	
Taxed	30	Tro'as	47, 48	Visibly	37		
Teachers	28	Tro gyl'li um	48	Vision	19	Zeal	21
Teaching	51	True	11	Visit	9	Zealously	41
Temperance	49	Trust	21	Vow	19, 49		

www.ingramcontent.com/pod-product-compliance
Lightning Source LLC
Chambersburg PA
CBHW020307170426
43202CB00008B/528